Praise for *Introduction to Knowledge Organization*

'The book uses a comprehensive theoretical framework for examining the theories of knowledge organization, the structural principles in knowledge organization, and the impacts of these theories and principles in the construction of knowledge organization systems (KOSs). A very unique component of the book is its coverage of the Semantic Web and linked data in the context of the representation of knowledge organization structures, including convincing cases and examples, as well as the issues and progress of fundamental and advanced applications. The range and scope of the book present a state-of-the-art review of the whole domain of knowledge organization.'
Marcia Lei Zeng, School of Information, Kent State University

'This is a broad and concise introduction to the growing field of knowledge organization. It introduces the most important kinds of knowledge organization systems used, both traditionally in physical libraries and in the digital world. It covers practical as well as theoretical and historical issues. I particularly like the view that the underlying theoretical assumptions of all knowledge organization systems need to be detected.'
Birger Hjørland, Department of Communication, University of Copenhagen

'This book provides a clear but detailed overview of knowledge organization. Its remarkable depth and analytical approach enables it to highlight useful connections between philosophical and theoretical approaches and practical applications. The author's classic interdisciplinary and encyclopedic knowledge makes it accessible both to a specialized and a general public. Searching first in its historical, philosophical and epistemological depths, Gnoli proposes a work that reads like a novel in spite of the details and technical terms. *Introduction to Knowledge Organization* will be suitable for established researchers, progressing and advanced students.'
Widad Mustafa El Hadi, Department of Information Science, University of Lille SHS

'In clear and accessible writing, for a broad group of readers regardless of their scientific field, Claudio Gnoli's new book introduces knowledge organization in a diachronic approach and presents the theoretical foundations and the practice in various contexts.
   Introduction to Knowledge Organization constitutes an exceptional contribution to the learning of knowledge organization, targeted at students, both undergraduates and postgraduates, and also at researchers.'
Olívia Pestana, Department of Communication and Information Sciences, University of Porto

'This well-written book is an excellent and timely account of the theories, practical applications and discipline of knowledge organization. This book quickly dispels any possible misconceptions that this area of library and information science is merely about arranging books on shelves. One of the book's many strengths lies in its very clear explanations of theories and topics. It also situates knowledge organization within its broader context, articulating the broader philosophical arguments at work. The inclusion of contemporary developments in knowledge organization research, as well as discussions about digital knowledge organization, make this book especially useful to those currently studying or working with knowledge organization. This book provides a highly informative account of the field of knowledge organization, and offers a powerful argument as to the importance, breadth and sheer usefulness of this significant area of library and information practice and research.

This book would be invaluable as a textbook for those studying library and information science (LIS), and would also be of interest to those working in knowledge organization and who want to enhance and deepen their understanding of knowledge organization.'
Deborah Lee, Department of Library and Information Science, City, University of London

Introduction to Knowledge Organization

Every purchase of a Facet book helps to fund CILIP's advocacy, awareness and accreditation programs for information professionals.

Introduction to Knowledge Organization

Claudio Gnoli

facet
publishing

© Claudio Gnoli 2020

Published by Facet Publishing
c/o British Library, 96 Euston Road, London NW1 2DB
www.facetpublishing.co.uk

Facet Publishing is wholly owned by CILIP: the Library and Information Association.

British Library Cataloguing in Publication Data
A catalogue record for this book is available from the British Library.

ISBN 978-1-78330-465-3 (paperback)
ISBN 978-1-78330-466-0 (hardback)
ISBN 978-1-78330-467-7 (e-book)

First published 2020

Typeset from author's files in 10/13pt Revival 565 and Frutiger by Flagholme Publishing Services.
Printed and made in Great Britain by CPI Group (UK) Ltd, Croydon, CR0 4YY.

For Sara Iommi (1983–2016), explorer of audiovisual archives, folk culture and knowledge at large, anthropologist, intellectual, militant, dearest friend.

Acknowledgments

I am grateful to David Bawden for his trust when proposing to produce this work. In revising its first version I have benefitted from knowledgeable comments and suggestions by Carlo Bianchini, Riccardo Ridi (all chapters), Ceri Binding, Amélie Daloz, Aida Slavic and Douglas Tudhope (individual chapters). My thanks go to my copy-editor Judith Oppenheimer for providing this non-native author with much help on English stylistic issues.

Contents

List of abbreviations

ASIS&T Association for Information Science and Technology
BC2   Bliss Bibliographic Classification, 2nd edition
BT   broader term
CRG   Classification Research Group
DDC   Dewey Decimal Classification
ILC   Integrative Levels Classification
ISBD   International Standard Book Description
ISKO   International Society for Knowledge Organization
KO   knowledge organization
KOS   knowledge organization system
LCC   Library of Congress Classification
LCSH   Library of Congress Subject Headings
LIS   library and information science
MARC   Machine-Readable Cataloging
NKOS   networked knowledge organization systems
NLP   natural language processing
NT   narrower term
OPAC   online public access catalog
OWL   Web Ontology Language
RDA   Resource Description and Access
RDF   Resource Description Framework
RT   related term
SKOS   Simple KOS
UDC   Universal Decimal Classification
UF   used for
URI   uniform resource identifier
XML   Extended Markup Language
W3C   World Wide Web Consortium

CHAPTER 1

Focusing the field

1.1 What is knowledge?

We all are aware that we are living in the Information Age, just as there have been ages of hunting and gathering, of agriculture and of industry in the preceding centuries and millennia. Information and knowledge shape our lives and our society in many ways.

This is now increasingly reflected in scholarship: terms such as *information architecture*, *knowledge management* and *knowledge representation* are increasingly common in the titles of conferences, books and educational programs. This book contributes yet another tile to this mosaic, by dealing with the conceptual arrangement of knowledge content.

However, before we get down to details we need to get a clear idea of what we are talking about. Obviously, this is a requirement in any domain, but it is even more necessary in the present case, as terms such as those used above, although suggestive, cover a particularly wide and fuzzy semantic space. When people from outside our field ask me about my research domain and I answer 'knowledge organization', their faces often express a mix of polite deference and perplexity about what exactly am I referring to.

Let us start with the first half of the term. What do we mean by *knowledge?*

1.1.1 Knowledge as representation of networks

Intuitively, we are aware that knowledge often refers to someone knowing something – that is, having developed some internal representation of certain external objects. That Maria knows the story of Christopher Columbus means that her mind has some representation of a sequence of events involving the navigator and his actions which led to the rediscovery of the Americas by Europeans.

The *representation* consists in a model of some set of entities and of links among them. While Columbus, his sailors, his maps and his ships were made of material substances, the notions in Maria's mind are immaterial ideas, recorded in a complex system of neural connections. Still, the material entities and the ideas modeling them are similar in terms of the network of relationships between their parts – they are isomorphic. Knowledge is thus a (usually simplified) reproduction of relationship networks in a different substrate. (This description differs from traditional philosophical definitions of knowledge as 'true and justified belief', although 'truth' corresponds in our description to isomorphism; a model that does not correspond to the represented object is a 'false' one.)

The exact relation between objects and their representation in knowledge has been the matter of philosophical discussion for millennia. Six centuries ago Nicholas of Cusa compared reality to the curvature of a circle, which human knowledge can try to approximate by designing polygons with an increasing number of sides, although without ever being able to achieve perfect circularity. Much more recently, philosopher of information Luciano Floridi (2019) has claimed that knowledge should be conceived of as being like cooking its objects – rather than just like depicting or photographing them. The resulting dish is very different from the original ingredients, although it does depend on them for its existence. The efforts of science are continually trying to get closer to a faithful representation.

In the above example the contents of Maria's mind exist in the brain of a living person. However, if we are talking about the knowledge contained in a locked library on a Sunday night, even though there is no living person there we can probably agree that there still is some knowledge. This seems to suggest that knowledge can exist even externally to people. So, can any entity be a carrier of knowledge?

Biologists have found that the DNA contained in cell nuclei transmits to the next generation some 'knowledge' about how an organism can develop, grow and work. Konrad Lorenz, a founder of the science of animal and human behavior, entitled his epistemological masterpiece *Behind the Mirror: a search for a natural history of human knowledge*. In chapter 1, on 'Life as a knowing process', he illustrates how the adaptation of an organism to its environment can be seen as a form of knowledge of the environment that has indeed been transmitted through its genes. The genes of a horse (through various biochemical stages) triggered the development of flat hooves, and that flat shape is adapted to the flat environment of the steppe where a wild horse will have to live, just as a sort of mold. So those genes are a form of knowledge of the flatness of the steppe (Lorenz, 1973).

1.1.2 Data, information, knowledge, understanding, wisdom

What Lorenz in this effective description calls 'knowledge' is nowadays more often described as *information*. These two terms are often used with overlapping meanings, and it has been found that the term 'information organization' is, to all intents and purposes, equivalent to 'knowledge organization' (Hjørland, 2012).

Their connection is better modeled in the metaphor of the *DIKW (data-information-knowledge-wisdom) pyramid* (Rowley, 2007; Frické, 2018): at the base of the pyramid, sets of integrated *data* form information; further integration of information gives rise to the upper layer of knowledge; and integration of knowledge can give rise to wisdom. Bawden and Robinson (2015) also proposed an additional level of *understanding* between knowledge and wisdom. In another metaphorical model (Marshall, 2013) information consists in isolated dots, while knowledge is a network of lines connecting certain dots and wisdom is the deletion of most dots and lines, keeping only those few elements that have proved to be most important.

As to the particular transition that interests us, that between information and knowledge, we can consider the representation of specific facts, such as 'Columbus sailed from Palos', or 'the steppe is flat', as information. The integration of many information elements into a connected, wider system gives rise to knowledge, such as 'the history of North America', or 'life in a steppe environment'.

If we hear about a dinner happening in Europe in 1453, this is one piece of information; but we can then compare this information with the broader network of our knowledge, which includes the notions that 1453 is before 1492, when Europeans first came into contact with native Americans, and that foods such as potatoes or tomatoes were imported into Europe only after the rediscovery of the Americas: from all this, we will *know* that that European dinner in 1453 could not have consisted of potatoes or tomatoes. Knowledge is a network of integrated information that allows us to process further information and set it in a broader picture.

The further integration of knowledge into understanding or wisdom is also very relevant, but concerns personal and spiritual development rather than techniques for arranging representations of reality, hence it is beyond the scope of this book.

1.1.3 Informational systems at various levels

As we have seen, information and its arrangement into networks of 'knowledge' (in a broad sense) can occur at several levels: not just cultural and cognitive, but also organic or even material.

Indeed, it is increasingly acknowledged that information in the most basic sense is a physical property that can be observed in any system, as it just accounts for how the system is and what its state is. The combination of the quantum numbers of an electron determines the range of its possible positions and movements around an atom's nucleus. Some are coming to think that information, in this sense, is even more fundamental than matter: before particles or waves, the world is comprised primarily of information and its structures (French, 2014).

These ideas are stimulating the development of a general 'philosophy of information' that can also be relevant (although not exclusively) to the field of library and information science (Floridi, 2002; Bawden and Robinson, 2017). A somewhat related conception is Charles Sanders Peirce's idea of 'thirdness' as a general ubiquitous relationship between any three entities. A typical example of thirdness is the relationship of 'semiosis', occurring between a sign, its object and its 'interpretant' (Peirce, 1934). According to Peirce, semiosis is not exclusive to human consciousness, but can occur among any three entities in the universe: in his conception, 'minds' exist at all levels of reality and the universe itself 'thinks'.

Such occurrence of signs at various levels reminds us of what we have said about representations occurring at several levels of organization. At the level of life, atoms and molecules are organized in ways that are specified by information contained in DNA and RNA to form organelles, cells, tissues, organs, organisms, colonies and populations. As we have seen, information plays a key role in genes, on which more complex biological systems depend.

At the next level, that of the mind (now meant in the typically human sense), information consists in notions that are acquired through the sense organs and learning, compared to innate logical faculties and processed in thought. Neural networks of information allow for the development of personal knowledge in individual organisms.

A further level is that of cultures developed by social beings, especially humans: in cultures, information is processed by gestures, languages and other symbolic systems that are transmitted through imitation and social learning. These can crystallize into artefacts, such as tools or buildings, and into 'mentefacts' (Gnoli, 2018b) – that is, intellectual products of human creativity, such as symphonies or theories.

As can be seen, each of these information levels can be based on the representation of the previous levels in some new form: organisms represent their material environment, such as the flatness of the steppe, by their adaptations as recorded in genetic information; minds represent an organism's internal and external situation to themselves; cultures represent mental, organic and material facts in their languages and symbols (Table 1).

Table 1 *Informational systems at different levels*

Informational systems		Varieties of information
cultures	mentefacts artefacts communities	public knowledge design gestures and words
minds		personal notions
life		adapted characters
matter		stable configurations
forms		logico-mathematical structures

If information at any given level is considered in the complex of its systemic connections, it can also be described as 'knowledge': so that Lorenz can say that a genome 'knows' its anticipated environment, or that a mind 'knows' the context in which the individual is standing.

However, the knowledge in which we are interested in this book is only that at the highest level, which is produced culturally in the form of mentefacts and is made available publicly (or potentially can be made available, such as files on a personal computer). This knowledge may be transmitted through oral traditions, or recorded in documents that can be reused later, even in the absence of the persons and societies that originally produced them, as is the case with Babylonian astrological texts or J. S. Bach's sonatas.

Such intellectual products have been described by philosophers as 'objectivated spirit' (Hartmann, 1953) or 'World 3', as distinct from 'World 1' of matter and 'World 2' of consciousness (Popper, 1978). Although they are based on the previous existence of organisms, of their minds and of social communities, once they have been produced mentefacts become independent entities with properties of their own. For example, as Popper observed, a certain theory can contain a logical implication, or a contradiction, that is identified only after the death of the theory's authors, leading to further consequences.

In time, the knowledge produced by human cultures forms a huge corpus, with many internal connections. However, not all potential connections between its parts are implemented, as they may have been produced by separate communities that were not aware of each other; some parts may even be at risk of eventually being lost if they are not properly transmitted and recorded. In order to enable the curation and exploitation of its full power, knowledge must be organized.

1.2 What is organization?

We now have to focus our attention on the second part of the name of our field. What exactly is *organization?*

In its most general sense, the notion of organization refers to structural connections between the elements of some system. Bricks can be thrown onto the ground randomly, in a disordered heap, or they can be organized in such a way as to form a wall. In the latter case, specific relationships are established among individual bricks: they are parallel to each other, they are arranged in rows, each row lying on top of the one below it, and so on.

The idea of organization is related to that of *order.* Order already is relevant in very basic sciences, such as mathematics and physics. For example, a series of numbers can form either an unordered set, which is usually notated between curly brackets: {5, 27, 3, 12} or an ordered set, which is notated between round brackets: *(3, 5, 12, 27).* As we shall see in Chapter 3, ordered series, or *arrays,* are a very important component in many knowledge organization systems.

To take another material example, a set of carbon atoms can be arranged randomly, or they can stand at a regular distance from each other in a repeating pattern, thus giving rise to a crystal of diamond. This example shows how important the consequences of order can be. Expressed in terms of thermodynamics, the disordered state is said to have greater entropy, while the ordered state has minimum entropy. Natural systems tend to evolve towards increasing entropy, that is, towards random dispositions of their elements, unless some external factor forces them into more ordered states.

Ordered arrangements of atoms can produce crystals of fascinating beauty, with smooth, bright surfaces. However, in the long term, order alone is not that interesting. If the Earth's surface were populated only with crystals it would be quite monotonous in comparison to the rich variety of complex organic and inorganic forms that we can see. This richness is actually possible because such forms are in states intermediate between maximum disorder (like the molecules of a gas) and maximum order (like the molecules of a crystal). Precisely stated, they are in *organized* states.

Organization is thus the arrangement of elements according to some structural principle which is not monotonous but changes only at certain points in some useful way. Bricks, rather than just being arranged in a straight, regular pattern that continues for meters, may be arranged to form corners, and be interrupted by gaps for doors and windows, so that they form the structure of a house. A house is not just ordered bricks: it is organized bricks.

The most interesting objects in our world are in fact organized objects.

1.3 What is knowledge organization (KO)?

Having discussed separately the two words composing the term for our field, let us put them together. Based on what we have said about each word, *knowledge organization* means the representation of real objects (knowledge) arranged into useful structures (organization). That is, the individual components of knowledge, like 'the history of North America', can be gathered and organized into more structured systems: say, a list of topics in the human sciences with relevant relationships between them, such as the relationship between the history of North America and that of Spain. The resulting complex system is called a *knowledge organization system*, often abbreviated as *KOS*.

KOSs prove to be very useful in many fields of human activity. The history of North America can be the subject of a TV program, as part of a series devoted to the Modern Age: a link to the whole series can then be offered on the broadcasting company's website, with individual subjects in the series arranged by some principle, such as day of transmission, or geographically, so that users can browse them easily. Additional connections can be offered, such as to programs in other series that are also related to North America in different ways (upcoming elections in Mexico, film festivals in Canada, etc.). Users can then navigate the website in intuitive ways, even without realizing that a KOS is part of its design.

A similar structure was part of the design of the famous 18th-century French *Encyclopédie*: although the articles were listed by alphabetical order, each one included references to other articles, and the references all together formed a precise scheme. The editors emphasized the role of links between knowledge elements in the article devoted to 'Encyclopedia' itself:

> In scientific treatises, it is the relations of ideas or phenomena which provide direction; as you advance, the subject matter develops, becoming either more general or more particular, according to the method chosen. The same will be true with respect to the general form of an article for the *Encyclopedia*, except that the dictionary or coordinated articles have advantages which in a scientific treatise can be achieved only at the expense of some quality; and it will owe these advantages to the references, the most important aspect of encyclopedic ordering.
>
> I distinguish two types of references: material and verbal. Material references illuminate the object, indicate its closest connections to others immediately related to it, and its distant connections with others that might have seemed remote from it; recall to mind common notions and analogous principles; strengthen consequences; bind the branch to the trunk, and lend to the whole the unity that so favors the establishment of truth and persuasion.
>
> (Diderot, 1755)

1.3.1 Personal and social knowledge

Individual humans accumulate personal knowledge by combining their innate knowing faculties with experience and learning from other humans. Personal knowledge can be organized in simple ways; for example, making a shopping list by store departments, arranging one's personal archive on shelves or in computer files and folders. Some of the organizing principles that we will review in the following chapters can also be applied at this simple level.

However, the need to organize knowledge grows as we move to socially shared knowledge. Indeed, if we call things only by a jargon known to us and our relatives this will not serve to communicate and coordinate action with other people. For such purposes some common 'vocabulary' and 'grammar' become necessary. Human communities have therefore developed shared symbolic systems, such as gestures, rituals, words, formulas, sayings, tales and myths.

At the societal level new forms of organization become relevant. For example, proverbs can summarize rich amounts of social knowledge in sayings that are easily learned and memorized; nursery rhymes often list familiar entities according to numerical order ('one is the Sun, two are the eyes ...'); folk taxonomies, as reflected in the lexica of dialects, convey practical knowledge about classes of relevant plants and animals. Until the Middle Ages most knowledge was taught in practical and oral forms even to learned students, and mnemotechnics allowed them to retain information by imagining such architectures as memory 'theaters', which organized it by rules of association.

All this is of potential interest to the domain of KO, but until now has been studied mostly by other disciplines, such as ethnography and ethnolinguistics. A study of the principles according to which gestural and oral forms of knowledge are structured is yet to be developed in the field to which this book is devoted. However, especially since the spread of printing techniques, knowledge has been transmitted increasingly in recorded forms (Ong, 1982), and KO has developed through the study of recorded documents.

1.3.2 Knowledge as recorded in documents

Both broadcasting company websites and encyclopedias convey knowledge, although in different forms. As we know, there are many other recorded sources of knowledge – especially nowadays – as diverse as journal articles, blog posts, messages, textbooks, posters, theater pieces, movies, etc. Collectively, they are called *documents*. Documents are packets of knowledge for public use that are conveyed in some material carrier.

While the most classic example of a document is a book, both older and newer document types also exist, from inscribed cave walls and clay tablets to DVDs and USB drives. The exact definition of *document* is not as plain as would at first appear: sometimes unusual objects are used as documents, such as Renaissance frescoed walls, or, in Lisbon, metro station walls on which sentences from texts by Portuguese writers are reproduced and which thus acquire a secondary function as documents.

Semioticians say that anything can be a sign as soon as it is considered to be one: clouds in the sky can be interpreted as a sign of changing weather, hence they become a 'document' about future weather. Anthropologists have a similar perspective concerning human products: 'All that is produced by a culture, either material or immaterial, transmitted intentionally or unintentionally, is a document: a book, as well as a table, a song or a landscape' (Iommi, 2019, 15–16; see dedication). However, a useful distinction can be made between objects designed to be documents from the beginning, like books or paintings, and objects used in that way only secondarily, such as clouds or murder clues (Buckland, 2014).

Borderline cases also exist. Living trees are usually not documents in the intentional sense, unless they are specimens cultivated in a botanical garden and labeled with their scientific names and additional information. While hiking with Sara Iommi in the Ligurian mountains, we found that panels had been installed by the Aveto Park staff describing the vegetation of the surrounding woodland – an extended version of specimen labels. Referring to our theoretical interests, the question arose whether, in this case, the whole wood had become a document. And, if so, where exactly did the document end? Or maybe the document consisted only of the panels? There are not always clear-cut answers.

1.3.3 Organizing public contents

To return to our main argument, modern KO is especially concerned with ordering knowledge as conveyed in some kind of document. But what is of interest to KO is not the document itself, be it a clay tablet or a website archive or a living tree. It is its knowledge content, such as the market sales recorded on the tablet, the history of North America discussed in the website or the ecology of the trees sampled as living specimens. What has to be organized is primarily knowledge contents, rather than external document features, although the latter will obviously affect their management (printed books can be kept in a library but living trees cannot; see section 2.4.3).

It will also be clear that the knowledge we are thinking of is the corpus of public knowledge as accumulated in collections of mentefacts (through the particular artefacts of documents), rather than the knowledge occasionally shared in a community or present in the mind of an individual person at any given moment.

Public knowledge clearly needs to be formalized by some common vocabulary, as different communities and different people often mean somewhat different things by the same words. The principles for performing such formalizations and recording the organized networks of links between parts of knowledge are a core object of KO.

Many disciplines and subdisciplines are called by names derived from Greek words. If we were to find one for our field, it could be *taxology*, that is, the science of how things can be ordered (from Greek *tássein* 'to arrange'). Some authors have indeed discussed these ideas using terms such as 'taxinomie' or 'taxilogie' (Grolier, 1974, 21, also citing Durand, 1899), but unfortunately these have not caught on. Scientific disciplines such as biology do designate as *taxonomy* their systematic branches, which are concerned with how the variety of phenomena can be arranged. However, what we mean to organize is knowledge about entities, rather than entities themselves. This could lead us to some neologism such as *sophotaxology* or *sophotaxis*!

In practice, however, the problems that we are considering have come to be increasingly identified as the field of *knowledge organization*, often shortened as KO. An awareness of the long history of KO practices, which we review in the next section (see especially 1.4.6), makes it advisable to adopt this term for the sake of consistency with the substantial amount of related literature and research.

1.4 A brief history of KO
1.4.1 KO in early civilizations

Although technologies evolve and allow for new ways of sharing and using information, all times and contexts have experienced a need for organizing their knowledge. Since the early times of recorded history, philosophers have sought the basic principles according to which a systematic framework of knowledge could be structured.

Ordering principles were also applied very early to the practical needs of organizing documents. In this case, the principles were less abstract, as the most ancient documents tended to deal with such everyday problems as trading products or ruling social life, rather than the general structure of the world (Santoro, 2015; Dousa, 2018).

The earliest-known written documents, Sumerian clay tablets and wax-covered wooden boards, are often structured as simple lists of items. Lists are indeed the minimal form of KOS, as we shall see in Chapter 3. They organize information elements into a limited, flat space that can be scanned in various directions by the reader. The adoption of writing thus encouraged people to organize their thoughts in newly systematic, more abstract ways (Goody, 1977). Although images painted on cave walls were already instances of documents, KO itself largely emerged from the rise of the written culture.

As the Mesopotamian civilization developed it also produced true libraries of clay tablets. Around 1100 BCE the Assyrian king Tiglath-Pileser I created a library that included works on divination, and also a kind of reference texts listing words, trees, animals, gods and places. Some 450 years later the famous Assurbanipal library in Nineveh was a rich collection of important texts – including the story of Gilgamesh and other literary works – where tablets were arranged systematically by subject in labeled jars that were themselves located on shelves and in storage rooms; tablets belonging to a series were also labeled on their outer side with the series title and a number. On the walls and doors of some rooms a catalog was carved, recording every title or incipit with the corresponding number of lines in a tablet, or the number of tablets in a whole work (Hyman, 1982, 7). Whether the whole library was organized by disciplines in the modern sense is disputed, although some rooms did specialize in historical, geographical, legal, grammatical or mythological texts.

A similar situation can be found in the remains of the other great culture of early antiquity: Egypt. Already around 2500 BCE lists of words, sometimes grouped into classes, can be found on clay tablets, and later, as was typical of this region, on papyrus rolls. Like in Mesopotamia, the listed items were not always *mutually exclusive* in a rigorous way, although they tended to be so in the special case of norms, according to which known facts had to be differentiated in a precise way in order to apply an appropriate sanction.

Vocabularies are better developed (Gardiner, 1947) in such Egyptian lexica as the *Ramesseum*, where words are formally enclosed between parallel lines and listed under classificatory headings; and even more so in Amenope's lexicon (around 1100 BCE, contemporary to Tiglath-Pileser I's library), where more than 600 items are classified under such main classes as:

I   Introductory heading
II   Sky, water, earth
III   People, court, offices, occupations
IV   Classes, tribes and kinds of human being
V   The cities of Egypt
VI   Buildings, their parts and earth types
VII   Lands, cereals and their products
VIII Beverages
IX   Parts of a cow and types of meat.

Within each class of this lexicon words can be further sorted according to such criteria as top to bottom (for classes II), general to specific (for classes III–IV and IX) or north to south (for class V). The basics of KO are there already!

The organization of knowledge that is found in encyclopedic works was not necessarily present in the organization of Egyptian libraries. Although some papyrus roll groups in the latter did concern a single discipline, such as magic, hardly any general systematic plans have been identified. However, in the library of the Temple of Horus at Edfu (3rd–2nd centuries BCE) inscriptions on the walls did catalog the rolls stored in 34 cases in a more systematic way, leading Grolier (1982) to describe it as the first library classification.

1.4.2 KO in the ancient East

As civilization progressed, lists of topics started to evolve into more general and abstract categories. Some of these were developed in the great civilizations of India and China.

According to the great Indian librarians Bhattacharyya and Ranganathan (1974, 121–2), 'the earliest of the schemes of Knowledge Classification known is the Vedic one'. This set of classical religious works, written in Sanskrit between 1500 and 800 BCE, includes as its four main classes:

- *dharma*, concerning 'the maintenance of society into a coherent organism' and corresponding to law, theology, ethics and sociology;
- *artha*, that is, 'the subjects leading to social wellbeing', corresponding to history, political science, economics and applied sciences;
- *kama*, 'the fulfilment of the involuntary creative urge in man, and/or for

the enjoyment of the results of such creation', corresponding to literature, fine arts and pure sciences; and
- *moksha*, which seeks 'to understand the universe by intellect and thereby get over the miseries of life', as in philosophy, or 'apprehends the totality of the universe, at once in its entirety, through intuition', as in spiritual experience (which Ranganathan put at the center of his own Colon Classification).

As can be seen, this arrangement is very different from those common in the modern West; it has a moral basis, by which increasingly elevating human practices are identified: 'To put it schematically, Exist → Grow towards full Happiness → Seek creative Joy → Attain ultimate Delight' (ibid.).

The Vedas also deal with a system of divinities which themselves represent general concepts of the natural world, and so are implicit main categories of Indian thought. These have influenced the later Indo-European divinities, such as those of ancient Persia and Greece – the god of lightning, of the sea, of time, etc. Babylonian cosmogony, *Enûma Eliš*, had already identified four basic elements: sea, earth, sky and wind, sometimes personified as four gods.

Moving to the most Eastern of the ancient civilizations, we come to China. Traditional Chinese philosophy identified two opposing principles or general categories: 'yin', meaning negative, receptive, wet, shady, winter or female properties, and 'yang', meaning positive, active, dry, bright, summer or masculine properties. Everything in Chinese culture is either yin or yang – or, more often, a combined interaction of the two. Yin is often represented by a broken line and yang by a solid line. This notation allows the combinatorial production of stacks of several lines (typically three – *trigrams*, or six – *hexagrams*, as listed in the ancient divination text *Book of Changes*). Every category can be used to divide them again: yang is thus divided into 'the yang of the yang' and 'the yin of the yang', and so on. A given concept, such as 'fire', corresponds to a trigram meaning 'the yang of the yin of the yang', and so on. All together, they yield a classification of all phenomena. As will be seen, the combination of fundamental elements is a typical procedure in KO. In this particular system, every hierarchical division is binary; that is, each class can be divided into only two subclasses.

As for library applications of KO, the earliest-known Chinese system is that describing the collections in the library of the Han emperor Cheng, in the first century BCE. A summarization of the texts could be found in a book known as the *Seven Epitomes*. Its main classes included 'the Six Arts', that is, classical works and commentary on them; 'the Masters' in literature and philosophy; 'lyrics and rhapsodies'; 'military texts'; 'divination and numbers'; and 'formulae and techniques' for health. Each class was further divided into subclasses. This system was influential in the following two centuries and was then replaced by such other catalogs as the *New List of the Central Collection of Classics* (Dousa, 2018).

1.4.3 KO in ancient Greece

While ancient Chinese thinkers found that everything is essentially dual, some Greek philosophers tried to establish monistic systems, founded on a single principle (*arché*), and debated about what such a principle was.

Around 600 BCE Thales of Miletus, considered to be the first philosopher in the typical rational, Western sense, claimed that such a principle was 'water'. His fellow citizen and scholar Anaximander opted for a more abstract 'unlimited' (*ápeiron*) principle, an original eternal mixture of everything, from which individual phenomena such as hot and cold, dry and wet, etc. are later distinguished (these are reminiscent of the Chinese dual categories, which also originate in a universal *qi* or *tao*). The younger scholar Anaximenes, on the other hand, called his first principle 'air' and claimed that by rarefaction it begets 'fire', while by condensation it begets winds, clouds, water, earth and stone. Democritus later claimed that the elements of reality are some *atoms*, a term literally meaning 'uncuttable': atoms move and combine in an immense number of ways to produce all material things (atomism was further developed by Epicurus and his Latin follower Lucretius). These philosophers thus tried to find some genealogical and hierarchical order between the substances that can be observed in nature.

With the emergence in the next centuries of the rational tradition of Socrates, Plato and Aristotle, the subjects of philosophical works started to be grouped systematically into certain 'arts', that is, disciplines. Aristotle wrote that these can be divided into *theoretical* arts, such as logic, mathematics, physics and metaphysics; *practical* arts, such as ethics, politics and economics (calling to mind the Vedic *artha*); and *poietical*, that is, productive arts, such as applied sciences and the fine arts. This classification is still influential in our modern Western categories, especially as it introduces the class of theoretical arts, knowledge sought for its own sake (as in modern 'pure' sciences), as opposed to knowledge applied to social life (the social sciences) or produced creatively (the humanities).

Aristotle's scholars, especially Theophrastus and Andronicus of Rhodes, started to organize the works of their polymath master according to a canonical order. This can still be traced in a term such as *metaphysics*, literally meaning 'the subjects coming after physics', where, in turn, *physics* means the sciences of nature (Greek *physis*).

Another fundamental contribution of Aristotle's is his list of the categories according to which things can be analyzed or predicated, as happens with the various indirect objects in a sentence. These were substance, quality, quantity, relative, place, time, posture, state, action and affection. Similar lists can still be found in the modern categories of facet analysis (see Chapter 3). Concepts can be distinguished into particulars (individuals) and predicates (classes), and the latter into universal predicates and dependent predicates, etc. These notions formed the skeleton of logic and ontology until Modernity.

Around 300 CE, in his introduction (*Isagoge*) to Artistotle's *Categories*, Porphyry wrote that things can be analyzed by a series of successive bifurcations, which all together produce a hierarchical *tree*: a substance can be either thinking or extended; extended substance can in turn be either inanimate or animate; animate beings can be either irrational or rational, like humans; humans can be either this or that; and that human can be an individual instance, e.g. Plato. Porphyry's Tree is another early example of a hierarchical classification. At the same time, the sequence of its divisions produces a series of increasingly higher forms, from inanimate beings to humans, later described as *scala naturae* (Ladder of Being; see Kleineberg, 2017): thus, later classes are at the same time more specific and occupy higher ontical levels (see 2.4.5) – a situation often rendering the term *hierarchy* ambiguous between the different meanings of specificity and of ranking.

Another KO achievement of the Greek culture was Callimachus' *Pinakes* (about 245 BCE), a lost 120-volume catalog of the famous library of Alexandria. For each work, it provided the title followed by biographical information about its author. It grouped works in six literary genres (rhetoric, law, epic, tragedy, comedy and lyric poetry) and five prose subjects (history, medicine, mathematics, natural science and miscellaneous works), each organized alphabetically by author.

1.4.4 KO in the Middle Ages

After the barbarian invasions, the dominance of the Graeco-Roman culture dissolved and became mixed with a variety of broader influences, including the monotheistic religions coming from the Near East. The works of Aristotle were enormously influential during the Middle Ages, when they merged with the Christian tradition into Scholastics.

Around 400 CE Martianus Capella was among the main developers of the system of Seven Liberal Arts, according to which medieval education was organized. In his encyclopedic *Marriage of Philology and Mercury*, mixing prose and verse, Capella described disciplines in an allegorical way as servants with which the bride, Philology (representing the love of study, as complementary to Mercury's profitable pursuit), is gifted: Grammar, Dialectic, Rhetoric, Geometry, Arithmetic, Astronomy and musical Harmony. Interestingly, two more arts also attend the wedding feast, Architecture and Medicine, but have to keep silent because they deal with earthly subjects, while the seven higher arts can speak to introduce their own contents. These characters could be remembered by pupils as mnemonic images for the corresponding fields, as was common in medieval education, which still used written knowledge to only a limited extent.

The first three of the seven arts came to be grouped in the *Trivium* of the literary arts as they were taught in the early European universities. The next four formed the *Quadrivium* of mathematical arts, including musical harmony, which also depends on numerical proportions (like the ratios among the distances producing successive notes along a lute string or a flute pipe).

Trivium's language and Quadrivium's mathematics are still the two fundamental disciplines in many primary schools, for which two basic types of exercise book are needed – ruled and squared. My master Eugenio Gatto observed that these layout structures tend to influence even our adult ways of thinking: squared structures are found in tables and databases, which encourage us to fill every cell with some content, although faceted subjects (see section 3.5) would be better represented in a ruled, language-like structure, as facets should never be mandatory elements (Gatto, 2006).

As for Aristotle's three divisions, they were simplified into two – theoretical and practical knowledge – by the early medieval philosopher Boethius. This influenced the systems of the following centuries, until time of the theologian and encyclopedist Hugh of St Victor (1096?–1141). To the theoretical and practical arts Hugh added the mechanical or 'illiberal' arts, including carpentry, weapons-making, commerce, agriculture, hunting, theatrics and medicine, which, unlike in Capella's system, were now entitled to be listed alongside the others. All of them are arranged by logic. Olson (2010) has discussed Hugh's relevance to KO; an interesting point is Hugh's awareness that a subject can be covered in more than one discipline, depending on the perspective from which it is considered: for example, commerce belongs to the mechanical arts, but is also connected with rhetoric because of the language skills used in negotiation – which are of even greater relevance in contemporary advertising! This anticipates the key idea of cross-references between different parts of a KOS.

Mnemotechnics, as enabled by Capella's metaphoric characters, was important again in the late Middle Ages. Catalan esoteric philosopher Ramón Llull listed nine basic 'attributes of God': goodness, greatness, eternity, power, wisdom, will, virtue, truth and glory; these could be represented by letters of the alphabet – an idea anticipating modern notational systems where a symbol corresponds to a concept and controls its position in lists (see section 3.3.1). Some years prior to this, Richard de Fournival had used letters of various styles and colors to represent classes of book subjects in his personal library in Amiens, France (Dousa, 2018, sect. 2.4.2).

In Llull's combinatorial technique the letters were written around a circle which could be rotated to match up with letters representing the categories in a second, concentric circle (difference, concordance, contrariety, principle, mean, purpose, majority, equality and minority). Combinations could be represented by pairs of letters. Llull thus emphasized the power of combining concepts to produce meaningful compounds, which is another classic device in KO. In his view, this allowed the principles of the sciences to be produced in a combinatorial way, and even to prove the truths of religion, so that everyone could understand them.

A similar idea was proposed in the 17th century by G. W. Leibniz, who envisaged the combination of basic concepts (e.g. 'animal' and 'rational') to produce compound concepts (e.g. 'human'). These would be represented by symbols, following the mathematical laws of algebra (e.g. 5 'animal' × 7 'rational'); in this way, any resulting concept (e.g. 35 'human') could be analyzed back to its prime factors, automatically producing such true statements as 'humans are rational' (as 7 is a factor of 35).

1.4.5 KO in early Modernity

Many other authors after Llull proposed or even produced systematic presentations of the knowledge elements that were available at their time, and of the terms used to represent them. They thus developed kinds of classification systems or thesauri (as they have been called since the time of P. M. Roget in the 19th century, see section 4.4.4).

Among them was Johann Heinrich Alsted, a follower of Llull and the influential French logician and pedagogue Ramus, and who was the teacher of Comenius and Johann Heinrich Bisterfeld. Bisterfeld (1605?–55), who was active in a Transylvanian academy (in modern Romania), appears to be of special interest to us, although he is as yet little known in KO literature. He developed a Philosophical Alphabet, using primary (or 'transcendental') terms to define the technical terms of all the sciences and representing their hierarchical relationships. This is reminiscent of our contemporary ontologies (see section 4.4.6). Terms that were common to all or most sciences allowed for the reconnection of the special sciences to a general system (Rossi, 2000).

Also common in the 17th century was the search for a 'philosophical language' that, unlike common languages, could represent the order and relationships of things by the form of its words (Laporte, 2017). Several projects of this kind were developed in England by Francis Lodowick, Thomas Urquhart, Cave Beck, George Dalgarno and John Wilkins (Maat, 2004). Of particular note is Wilkins' *Essay towards a Real Character and a Philosophical Language* (1668), which also included an original writing system and has rightly been described as an ancestor of modern classification systems (Vickery, 1953) – despite Jorge Luis Borges' (1952) famous ironical account of it. For example, $n\eta k$ 'whole-footed terrestrial beasts' was a subdivision of $n\eta$ 'terrestrial beasts', which in turn was a subdivision of n 'beasts'.

Contemporaneously, naturalists and the curators of museums and botanical gardens faced the need to organize growing quantities of specimens and the knowledge about many new plants, animals and minerals collected from exotic lands during voyages of discovery in Africa, Asia and the Americas. People like bibliographer and botanist Conrad Gessner (1516–65) searched for criteria by which to organize collections and works about them, and started to develop *taxonomies*, that is, hierarchical trees of all varieties of natural items, by which their *types* could be identified and named and their supposed relationships with other species could be expressed.

Any new plant or animal has a large number of *characters*, some of which resemble those of certain known species and some of which resemble others: which characters are to be considered as primary, in order to develop a taxonomy? Experience gradually led naturalists to understand that certain characters, for example the reproductive organs or the skeleton, were especially meaningful as they implied whole, interconnected anatomical structures, rather than being just a detail. The Swedish botanist Carl von Linné (1707–78) famously developed a more advanced *Systema Naturae*, including taxonomies for plants, animals and minerals, which today remains the basis for modern botanical and zoological nomenclature.

1.4.6 Classification in modern libraries

Taxonomies enabled the organization of knowledge in these special sciences, but did not consider the relationships between different sciences, nor their general order. These problems were addressed by Francis Bacon (1561–1626), who argued for the connection and unity of all the sciences. Bacon aimed to correct the false beliefs that originated from the common uses of language, although in his view the practice of definitions, as in philosophical languages, was not the solution but merely a shifting of the problem. He thus preferred an empirical approach, which anticipated that of modern science.

Bacon classified 'the parts of human learning' according to the different faculties of 'man's understanding': sciences of memory, sciences of imagination and sciences of reason. This tripartition had a lasting influence, through the French encyclopedists, the US president Thomas Jefferson and the librarians E. W. Johnston and W. T. Harris, to Melvil Dewey, who followed it (in reverse order: reason, imagination, memory) in 1876 to list the main classes of his Decimal Classification (Sales and Pires, 2017; Dousa, 2018, sect. 2.6.4).

Librarians had already been organizing their books by subject areas, but their subdivisions were very broad ones, such as *Theology*, *Philosophy* or *Literature*; additionally, their internal subdivisions tended to depend on the accidental sizes of shelves and rooms, or on the sizes of the books themselves (very large books tended to be shelved together, for practical reasons). Within each broad subdivision the order of the books depended simply on the sequence of their acquisition by the library.

The invention and spread of printing led to an exceptional increase in the number of books that libraries had to deal with, and the broad subdivisions no longer sufficed to remember where a book on a particular subject could be found. Librarians now needed to rely more on catalogs, which had to be more accurate and consistent by following codified rules, such as those formulated by Antonio Panizzi for the library of the British Museum in London.

During the 19th century detailed systems for the classification of subjects were developed in France by the bibliographer Jacques Charles Brunet, and in Germany by some librarians. The system devised by Andreas Schleiermacher for the Ducal Library in Darmstadt was particularly advanced, and already had various key features of our contemporary systems (Stevenson, 1978).

One such was *relative location*, which consists in determining classmarks according to the subject of each particular book, independently of the shelf where it is located. That is, what is labeled is the book itself, rather than the shelf. This simple idea meant a great deal for the organization of subjects, as new books could now be given shelfmarks similar to those of existing books on related subjects and thus be shelved together with them, rather than according to the available space. To accommodate a new book on the shelves, it was enough simply to slightly shift the existing books to the right, or onto the next shelf, without having to change their marks. Another remarkable benefit was that if the entire collection had to be moved to different shelves, rooms or even buildings, there was no need to change the label on the spine of every book, nor its classmark in the catalog.

These innovations were also adopted in the major American libraries, which were becoming the international leaders towards the end of the 19th century. For the most important of them, the Library of Congress in Washington, DC, Hanson and Martel devised a system (derived from Charles Ammi Cutter's Expansive Classification) that was still partially tied to the physical location of the books: indeed, class headings in the Library of Congress Classification have notations such as *LB1705–2286* for 'education and training of teachers and administrators', meaning that books on these topics are located from shelf *1705* to shelf *2286*, not allowing for indefinite expansion or moving the collection.

To manage relative location, a clever innovation was introduced by Melvil Dewey when he was a young librarian at Amherst College in New York. With his *decimal* notation, every subject class could be divided into ten more specific subclasses, represented by digits *0* to *9*, which in turn could be divided into ten sub-subclasses, and so on. As with decimal numbers, every additional digit represents additional specificity, so that books on any subject can be shelved mechanically just after those treating a slightly more general topic.

Dewey's Decimal Classification was imitated by many subsequent systems, including the Universal Decimal Classification (UDC) developed by the Belgian lawyers Paul Otlet and Henri La Fontaine. Their UDC was aimed at organizing a vast bibliography of the literature published all around the world, indexed on standard cards and kept in immense file cabinets at their Institut international de bibliographie in Brussels (which later evolved into the Fédération internationale de la documentation, FID). Otlet, a pioneer in the new science of documentation, obtained permission from Dewey to reuse his scheme in a modified version, including a number of *common auxiliaries*, that is, suffixes in the notation which can add specificity to any subject by appending standard symbols for places, periods, document types, etc. (see section 3.5.4).

This practice, already used by Schleiermacher, opened the door to the development of more *synthetic* systems, such as that by Julius Otto Kaiser (using terms rather than symbols), and especially the Colon Classification of S. R. Ranganathan, which adopted a full analysis of subjects into *facets* that can be combined to produce synthetic classmarks. Facet analysis was subsequently acknowledged to be the best way to produce effective classification systems, as claimed in a famous paper by the Classification Research Group (CRG, 1955), and was gradually introduced into existing systems. Also of special importance is Henry Evelyn Bliss's Bibliographic Classification, which was completely revised by the British CRG into a fully faceted system, BC2.

Bliss Bibliographic Classification is also an important application of a different principle for deciding the order of main classes: *gradation in speciality*. This resulted from the views of many philosophers, especially Auguste Comte, who ordered the sciences not according to the human knowledge faculties, as Bacon did, but according to how specific to certain objects they are. In this approach, philosophy and mathematics are listed first because they apply most generally to all studied objects – one can develop mathematics of stars, or of economy, or of anything; these are followed by physics and chemistry, which deal with more specific aspects of things; then by biology, which deals only with the living phenomena (there is no biology of squares or of electrons); then psychology, which deals with the mind as a specific manifestation of life; then sociology (the new science on which Comte focused), which deals with society as a peculiar manifestation of the human mind (Comte, 1854).

This order of the sciences corresponds to the order of their objects in a series of *integrative levels*: from particles through atoms, molecules, cells, organisms and populations to minds, societies and their cultural products – recalling the medieval *scala naturae* or Ladder of Being (Kleineberg, 2017; see section 2.4.5). Besides Bliss Classification, these levels can also be traced in the main classes of James Duff Brown's Subject Classification, Ranganathan's Colon Classification, Dahlberg's Information Coding Classification and many others.

Dewey Decimal Classification remains the most widespread system across the world, such that, independently of its merits and limitations, it has become an international reference for specifying subject matter. When different cultures have needed to devise classmarks according to their own uses not common in the West, the decimal structure of Dewey has still been a starting point for adaptation, producing, for example, the Korean Decimal Classification and the Nippon Decimal Classification (see section 2.4.4).

In other countries, where the basic organization of Dewey was not acceptable for strong ideological reasons, completely different systems have been developed: the main classes of the Russian Library-Bibliographical Classification (also known as BBK: Sukyasian, 2017) and those of the Chinese Library Classification (Bu, 2017) reflect socialist doctrine, placing Marxism and Leninism at the beginning of the scheme, rather than philosophy and religion as in Dewey and its derivatives.

1.4.7 KO in the digital age

In the second half of the 20th century documentation techniques underwent enormous changes: information was now recorded in standard formats and retrieved by mechanical techniques, such as punched cards, computers and networks. Any word or other symbol could now be retrieved from huge databases, functioning in the same way as a *keyword* does in internet search engines. This led many to think that there was no longer any need for intellectual indexing of subjects (Dextre Clarke and Vernau, 2016).

This approach can indeed work well to extract such non-common terms as person or place names. But anyone searching for a topic represented by very common words, expressed by many synonyms or discussed in different languages will have experienced the frustrating results of such unrefined methods, and it is soon understood that the old techniques of KO are still very useful if coupled with digital technologies, rather than the digital technologies being treated simply as an alternative to them.

Thus, new kinds of KOSs have been developed for use in computer-based contexts (see section 4.4). Words to be searched have been organized into thesauri (Dextre Clarke, 2017) in which the terms available for searching are listed with their synonyms, hypernyms, etc., or more generally into *controlled vocabularies*. Less formal taxonomies have been reintroduced in information architecture, e.g. to map the contents of a website and to provide its users with menus and other navigational tools. Web interfaces and social networks allow users to contribute further terms that are more familiar to them, thus participating in the development of a *folksonomy*. Terms, and the concepts they represent, can also be manipulated by computers in automatic ways, provided that they are expressed in strictly formal ways as in *ontologies*.

As we shall see in the following chapters, all these new kinds of systems are just different implementations of the same basic principles. What changes is just their syntax, format and semantic richness, which will be reviewed in Chapter 4. These rapid developments have produced a very wide variety of initiatives – making KO practices popular, but often calling similar things by different terminologies. This, unfortunately, can mean a big waste of effort, despite the increasing amount of investment in information technology and management. All this variation is much in need of being reconnected to a common framework.

Today, the chief hope for consistency resides in the more general, encompassing notion of *knowledge organization*. This term had already been used in the titles of two important books by Bliss (1929; 1933), but was rediscovered in 1989 after the German Classification Society became dominated by mathematical-statistical approaches. This led a small group of researchers who were still interested in the intellectual side of classification to found a new association. To avoid similarity to the old name, they called it the International Society for Knowledge Organization (ISKO) and changed the title of their journal, published since 1974, from *International Classification* to *Knowledge Organization*.

Propelled by the strong motivation of its first president and editor-in-chief, Ingetraut Dahlberg (1928–2017; see Ohly, 2018), ISKO has consolidated over time and spawned a number of regional chapters, including those of the German-speaking area, Spain–Portugal, France, Italy, the UK, North America, Brazil, Singapore, the Maghreb, West Africa, etc. Chapters hold regional and international conferences on a regular basis and their members often contribute to the journal, the KO literature and the online *ISKO Encyclopedia of Knowledge Organization*, founded by Birger Hjørland, another important theorist in the field.

All this makes ISKO a useful international reference for the diversified field of the conceptual organization of knowledge, although its centrality by no means gives it a monopoly. Indeed, relevant research and applications in KO are also produced in such other journals, associations and conferences as *Journal of Documentation*; *Cataloging and Classification Quarterly*; the (originally American) Association for Information Science and Technology (ASIS&T) and its *JASIST* journal; *Journal of Applied Ontology* and other titles; the biennial UDC Seminars (since 2007); the ongoing NKOS (Networked Knowledge Organization Systems) Workshops; and various university laboratories and companies around the world. An updated list of relevant events and publications can be found on the ISKO home page (www.isko.org).

CHAPTER 2

Theories of knowledge organization

2.1 Theories are needed

In everyday life we use many kinds of KO systems without reflecting about it. We quickly browse menus in a pizzeria or services on a government website without paying attention to the fact that they are sorted by some principle: pizzas may be listed by increasing price, by ingredients or in alphabetical order; public services may be ordered according to the different life stages (services for children, for occupations, for old people and so on) or by the offices and departments dealing with them.

A famous book on information architecture (Krug, 2014) is titled *Don't Make Me Think!* It represents a view common among interface designers: users should not waste their time in understanding which KO principles have been adopted, but should use them in intuitive ways to quickly get to the content they need. This is correct from a functional viewpoint. After all, we do not need to know how a watch works before acquiring the only information relevant to us: what time it is.

However, as we are now considering KO we have to delve into its mechanisms. Think of those watches with transparent cases that were once fashionable, allowing one to see their mechanisms while providing time information remained their main function. Why not offer knowledge organized in effective ways, and at the same time allow curious users to peer into the mechanism and understand how and why is it organized in those ways?

The mechanisms of KO are its structuring principles and devices, which we will treat in the next chapter, while the theories that inform them are the topic of this chapter. Like the watch mechanism, theories and devices are often non-explicit. Still, they exist and are necessary, because any way of organizing knowledge implies some theory of knowledge and its structures.

Clare Beghtol, an important writer on KO theory, contrasted the systems developed for the retrieval of already available knowledge, which are based on explicit principles developed by experts in KO, with the 'naive' systems that organize new knowledge and are developed by people with no particular interest in KO (Beghtol, 2003). Hjørland and Nicolaisen (2004) replied to this that the contrast is only apparent, because even 'naive' systems are based on some principle. No system can be truly atheoretical (Hjørland, 2016).

One of the tasks for KO scholars is to analyze which theoretical principles underlie each system, and to discuss the merits and problems of each. This critical approach has become more prominent as KO develops into a mature field of research rather than being just a set of empirical techniques that have been found to work well in libraries or in computer science. It is now claimed that any KOS, whether old or new, is a cultural product and needs to be deconstructed to detect its underlying theoretical assumptions. Such 20th-century philosophers as Ludwig Wittgenstein, Thomas Kuhn and Michel Foucault have been very influential in advising scholars that any cultural phenomenon can be analyzed in this way.

In some academic circles this has even become a fashion in itself, leading people to think that uncovering theoretical assumptions is the only task of KO, and that no one KOS is better than any other. This kind of cultural relativism is obviously an extreme position, as its ultimate conclusion would be that any particular KOS will do, and the task of developing new ones is irrelevant. I believe that there are indeed KOSs that are better than others, and that there are reasons why this is so.

At the same time, we need to avoid naive scientism, uncritically assuming that some particular KOS is good and completely satisfactory. As we saw in section 1.4, KO involves a perennial human search for the most appropriate, useful and up-to-date systems. It will therefore be useful to start our journey into KO by focusing on theoretical assumptions and reviewing various alternative theoretical approaches.

2.2 From percepts to concepts

As we saw in section 1.1, knowledge tries to model the complexity of reality by representing it in simplified ways. Our first means of knowing reality is through the sense organs and innate categories (such as causation or time), which convey information on some aspects of the environment to our brain. Our access to reality can never be direct, so to speak, but is necessarily mediated by our human condition.

The philosophers Immanuel Kant and Arthur Schopenhauer called reality in itself the *noumenon*, from a Greek word meaning 'conceived'. They emphasized that we cannot know it, as what we actually know (besides our own knowing mechanisms) are only *phenomena*, again from a Greek word, meaning 'what appears'. (Only mystics try to directly contemplate reality as a whole. But KO does not deal with this approach; rather, it tries to examine how reality is articulated in particular structures and to model these structures.)

Reality in itself and phenomena are the first two *dimensions* of our knowledge: we will label them with the Greek letters α and β, respectively. We will later identify further dimensions of knowledge; for now, we can observe that, not having direct access to reality in itself (α), KO has to begin its task with phenomena (β).

How do phenomena come to us through our cognitive apparatus? What the sense organs first transmit to our brain are *percepts*. For example, I perceive a cloth of a particular shade of blue as my visual sense organs and brain react to particular electromagnetic frequencies in the light reflected by the cloth; or I perceive a high temperature when close to a flame as my thermal receptors react to the heat. The sense organs and brain select only some aspects of reality (those that are likely to be most useful for our survival, as a result of the evolution of our cognitive apparatus) and neglect others, such as the infrared or ultraviolet frequencies of light (Rogers, 2017).

However, percepts are not the end result of cognition. Indeed, our brain combines various percepts, on the basis of both innate and learned rules, to build a more consistent and complete image of the external world. This process already is an unconscious form of KO, as acknowledged by Ranganathan (1967, 77, sect. CP2):

> Classification in Sense 2 is inherent in Man. Perhaps it is a concomitant of the finiteness of the speed of neural impulses in the human body. When the speed is finite, structure emerges. Wherever there is structure, sequence emerges. When sequence is helpful to the purpose on hand, it is Classification. The sequence inevitable inside the skin, so to speak, gets expressed extraneurally also. To classify in Sense 2 is thus a neural necessity.

In this way every human being perceives and organizes many things, gradually accumulating sensorial information. A new percept can then be compared with the personal memory of previous percepts, developing a corpus of experience.

Additionally, humans share information between them through gestures and language – probably their most peculiar ability, as compared to other animals. As a result, individual perceptions and memories are compared and integrated with those of other humans into a collective corpus of knowledge. In order to be available publicly, knowledge has to be transmitted by oral traditions or to be recorded in more stable ways in documents.

When we perceive a fire we can compare this percept to our instincts, our experience and publicly shared knowledge, all indicating that fire is hot and dangerous, even without any need to touch it personally. Thus, our percept of a bright, flickering flame is (1) integrated into a consistent image of a flame, (2) compared to our previous experience of other flames, (3) compared to our innate fear of burning things and (4) compared to our socially learned knowledge of fire. The percept has been translated into a *concept* – the concept 'fire'. (Concepts are denoted by quotation marks.)

Concepts are not just perception or sparse information: they are knowledge. Indeed, Dahlberg (1978) has identified concepts as the basic units of knowledge. A concept is a class of individual phenomena grouped on the basis of both individual percepts and their processing through personal and collective experience. The concept 'fire' is the class of all instances of bright, hot, flame-like, etc. phenomena as perceived by members of a certain culture.

The collective component can be best observed in certain concepts, such as 'blue': although it is ultimately derived from real electromagnetic radiations, 'blue' also depends on the particular way that our culture segments the electromagnetic spectrum, as different cultures distinguish a different number of colors; so people of another culture may, for example, consider 'dark' the same light frequency that we consider 'blue'. In the same way, Arctic people may be used to distinguishing between different shades of 'white', just as Londoners are used to distinguishing between various kinds of 'rain'. The classification of colors is a famous case in the discussion of objectivity and cultural relativity in KO (Berlin and Kay, 1969). On the other hand, such concepts as 'fire' seem to be more easily categorized in the same ways across cultures.

Of course, the most common way that cultures identify and share concepts is through words. The word *fire* conveys the concept 'fire' among English speakers. Words, and languages in general, are thus very important for KO (see section 3.1). However, words are not the same as concepts. Different languages denote 'fire' by other words (*feu, fuoco,* etc.). And the same English word *fire* can also mean other concepts, such as 'shoot' or 'dismiss'.

This is the chief reason why crude word search is not enough in information retrieval and KOSs are needed: a large part of their functionalities deal with the complex relationships between words and concepts. These also include the influence of words on conceptualization: cultures that lack a specific word for 'blue' may tend to lump this concept with a more generic concept of 'dark', and so on.

2.3 Bottom-up and top-down procedures
Once concepts have been identified and listed, we can start to organize them into more complex structures – that is, to do KO in the proper sense.

As some concepts, like 'color', are more general than others, like 'blue', one has to decide whether to start from very general concepts and divide them into more specific ones, thus following a top-down strategy; or, doing things the other way around, to group specific concepts into increasingly general categories. There are various views on this. However, as Rick Szostak observes, in practice both strategies are followed in a complementary way when developing KOSs.

The top-down approach is particularly important in classical logic. One can start from what used to be called 'the universe of knowledge', as it can be represented, for example, in all the topics covered in a general library or in a general encyclopedia. This also implies a most general concept, like 'universe' or 'world', that encompasses all specific concepts.

Such a top class must then be divided into most general subclasses, as in the ancient Indian and Chinese systems mentioned in section 1.4.2. Very general classes are often called *categories*. In the binary system of the *Book of Changes* the top categories are 'yin' and 'yang'. These are further divided into sub-subclasses (second-order categories), and so on. In the Western tradition originating with Aristotle, this procedure is known as *logical division* (Frické, 2016): in its typical application of Porphyry's Tree the top class is 'substance', which is divided into 'thinking' and 'extended'; the latter is further divided into 'inanimate' and 'animate', and so on.

While such general categories are usually identified by philosophers according to quite abstract bases, scientists often work with more specific concepts and try to organize them from the bottom up into increasingly general classes. Taxonomists of plants, animals and minerals start with concepts like 'lion' or 'silver' and group them into such general classes as 'carnivores' or 'metals', then group these into more general ones like 'mammals', 'chemical elements', etc.

Hopefully, philosophers starting from the top downwards and scientists starting from the bottom upwards should meet somewhere in the middle and collaborate to build a consistent scheme encompassing all concepts. In practice, however, their projects often pursue different aims, so that philosophers are interested in only the top categories and disregard the trivial details of everyday entities, while scientists prefer to stay 'scientific', without speculating too much about general categories. The most complete systems, like Wilkins' Real Character or Bliss Bibliographic Classification, are especially interesting for KO just because they combine both general and special concepts.

In library and information science both methods are followed. The bottom-up method prevails in subject headings and thesauri, which start from terms representing specific concepts and group them under increasingly broader terms, while the top-down method prevails in bibliographic classifications, which divide knowledge into increasingly specific sectors.

Some modern classificationists, such as Jason Farradane (1950) and Derek Austin, have argued that even classification should start from the bottom up, so as to express specific concepts in a more flexible way and avoid a priori categorizations. However, when it comes to organizing these specific concepts into a complete scheme, some general categories such as 'objects', 'processes', 'properties', or 'matter', 'life', 'mind', 'culture' are still needed. It seems that in order to deal with KOSs in a complete way we have to consider both philosophy and the special sciences.

2.4 The dimensions of knowledge

Listing and organizing concepts may be enough for such tools as a thesaurus or a dictionary, both of which deal with individual terms. However, most knowledge sources, such as a lecture, a documentary movie, a monograph or the program of a university class, have complex subjects. While a definition of *fire* in a dictionary simply refers to the concept 'fire', a book or a movie dealing with fire will discuss relationships among many different phenomena that are related to fire in various ways – say, chemical reactions, melting of metals, rescue services, etc. In the words of Douglas Foskett (1958, 2),

> their subject matter consists of bits of knowledge about natural phenomena. What we have to arrange, therefore, is actually knowledge of natural phenomena, though it is usually represented by marks on pieces of paper. [... T]hey contain descriptions of objects in relation to one another.
>
> To give you one simple example. The classification of objects in a natural history museum enables us to detect identity between several objects. Each object has its own place, arrived at by a process of logical division, *per genus et differentiam*. By this means we can locate a dinosaur or a blue rag. But consider 'the corrosion of tinplate by acid fruit products' or 'the Direct method of teaching French in secondary modern schools'. What genus can be said to contain each of these? What characteristics of division distinguish them? Where you would put them in a museum?

These situations introduce additional layers into our discourse, besides that of phenomena, which concern the particular ways (that we will call *perspectives*) in which related phenomena are connected and discussed, the material carriers where this happens, how such resources can be used, and so on. A plate as displayed in a museum in not the same thing as a plate discussed in a book or in a handicraft lesson, each with its network of links to related subjects (although, obviously, being related to them).

Let us briefly enumerate this sequence of *dimensions*, as they are called by Hartel and Hjørland (2003) and Gnoli (2016), before discussing the relevance of each for theoretical approaches to KO:

- α *reality* in itself, only indirectly known through our sense organs and learning;
- β *phenomena*, e.g. 'fire', 'melting', 'rescue services', as they have been identified in the collective accumulation and development of knowledge over time;
- γ *perspectives*, e.g. 'alchemy' or 'industrial chemistry', as ways to look at a set of phenomena from particular viewpoints and for particular purposes;

- δ *documents*, e.g. 'documentary movie', as carriers recording knowledge about certain phenomena from a certain perspective;
- ε *collections*, e.g. 'movie library', gathering large sets of documents for a specific cultural mission;
- ζ *information needs* e.g. 'historical research', as they motivate a particular user to search and exploit certain collections;
- η *people*, e.g. 'French female 24-year-old PhD student', as they bring their personal skills and experience to addressing a certain information need;
- θ *cognition*, e.g. 'browsing ability', as an innate human skill affecting the way people express their needs and interact with collections.

Each of these dimensions of knowledge is particularly addressed in specific disciplines: perspectives are addressed in epistemology, collections in library or museum science, people in sociology, cognition in cognitive science. However, they all participate in the determination of a specific instance of knowledge use, like 'browsing by a French student doing historical research in a movie library owning documentaries on industrial chemistry about melting'. Therefore, KO should account in some way for all of them when stating its principles and systems.

The various theories of KO have particularly emphasized one or another of these dimensions. We will thus review each dimension in order to show the different kinds of approach that can be taken. Ideally, in order to develop a full account of KO problems, the contributions of each dimension should be compared and all integrated.

2.4.1 User-based approaches

Let us start from the bottom of our list and proceed upwards. In other words, we are starting from the cognition (θ) of actual individual people (η) who can use and process knowledge as they experience various information needs (ζ).

It has become common to claim that information services should be centered on users. This is partly a reflection of the evolution of computer science. In the 1970s and 1980s early applications of computers to information search and retrieval were possible only through quite complex procedures, such as formulating queries in some special command-line language. Subsequently we have seen the gradual introduction of *user-friendly* graphical interfaces, hypertexts and multimedia (Ridi, 2017). As communication technologies have pervaded more and more aspects of our work and life, experts have emphasized that tools should be designed with the lay user in mind. This has now been implemented in many ways, although sometimes at the risk of forgetting the basic meanings and structures of the content itself.

It has become fashionable to argue that knowledge should be organized according to particular end-user groups and their purposes. While in principle this is a fair aspiration, in practice it is not always feasible, as a set of resources that are organized for one particular user group will necessarily neglect others. This suggests a role for standardization not as a means to impose any particular culture on users but as a common language allowing different communities to use the same resources and to communicate.

Clearly, specific projects may be targeted to serve particular groups, e.g. by age (children, young people, adults, old people), by gender, by language spoken, by level of education, by culture. One example is online public access catalogs (OPACs) or other bibliographic discovery tools designed in such a way as to encourage children to explore library or museum collections. They may be based on easy, colorful menus and search interfaces rich in cartoon-like icons. Some libraries have even developed faceted systems (see section 3.5) so that a child can start by selecting 'a tale' rather than an illustrated book, then browse a menu including 'monster tales', 'fairy tales' and 'animal tales', and so on; a further facet may allow the selection of age groups, resulting in the display of a list of suitable books.

There is a related idea behind the theory developed in some German libraries (Emunds, 1976) that books can be recommended to public library users in three stages: a first room with a selection of new or popular books, which are brought to the attention of general readers by non-disciplinary 'fields of interest'; a second section with books in common usage arranged on open shelves; and a store with specialized and less-frequently used books. Over time, books may be moved from one section to another, depending on their age and on usage statistics.

In the above examples the subject matter of a document is not adopted as a basis for structuring the collections, but is subordinated to categories of use, either occasional or professional, and of users (more or less old, educated, etc.).

Categories of people (η) are analyzed in the discipline of sociology, so people-based approaches may build on sociological studies of potential users. However, even the same person may encounter different information needs at different times: they may need a complete bibliographic search when researching their degree thesis, but may also look for a beautiful story to relax with while on vacation, or for a practical manual on growing tomatoes on their balcony during leisure time. The dimension of information needs (ζ) thus needs to be distinguished from that of people, and not to be completely determined by the latter.

Information needs lead people to behave in certain ways when searching knowledge bases by following some (more or less conscious) strategy: for example, doing a quick search or a more methodical one, evaluating the first results and refining the strategy accordingly in a feedback process. They may opt for searching the closest available neighborhood library, or for navigating online through long paths and travelling to suitable information services until they find the best resources.

Hjørland (2013) associates user-based approaches to KO with the theoretical field of cognitive science; indeed, many studies have analyzed user samples by focusing on their cognitive abilities when searching for information. In Hjørland's view, this implies the adoption of a universalist paradigm, as the minds of users are considered to be representative of some universal mental mechanisms that are common to all humans, and have often been modeled by analogies with the mechanisms of computers. This view was especially common in the last two decades; recently it has been replaced by a more socially oriented paradigm focusing instead on the differences between the cultures and communities to which users belong, so that no general rule can be assumed for all users.

On the other hand, Marcia Bates, who has written much on the information-seeking behavior of users, has observed that the social status of users is just as important a factor as their universal human nature. As humans have both a biological nature (θ) and a personal history of individual and cultural experiences (η), she recommends 'to integrate the social and cultural with the underlying biological and physical anthropological layers of human experience with respect to information seeking and searching' (Bates, 2002).

Indeed, biological and anthropological layers do affect information needs in certain ways. For example, human cognition is known to be able to browse only a limited number of items at one time. Blair (1980) found that the average user is willing to browse around 30 items in a list, known as their *futility point*, before giving up or changing their strategy; even when search engines report having found millions of results for our keyword searches, it shows only the first ten – the remaining results will be displayed only if the user is motivated to click on the links to subsequent pages.

For this reason, a KOS may list subjects in arrays of only five to ten elements (following 'the magical number seven, plus or minus two', as identified by Miller, 1956); if more items have to be listed, they can be grouped conveniently in a smaller number of more general classes to allow for their easy exploration in subsequent hierarchical steps. This principle is now well known to information architects, who recommend that web designers should find a good balance between the number of items listed at each step (not too great, in order to be browsed easily) and the depth of a hierarchy (which can force users to follow complex paths through many steps) before coming to a suitable specific class, thus countering the other principle of *least effort* (Bates, 2002). The ideal hierarchy should be neither too flat nor too deep.

2.4.2 Collection approaches

What users materially search are collections (ε) of information resources kept and managed in some private or institutional facility.

Theory of KO was developed in the 20th century especially based on experience in libraries, where huge numbers of books and descriptions of them have been accumulated (Dousa, 2018). However, awareness has increased that similar basic principles can also be applied to other kinds of collections, such as archives, museums and galleries (grouped with libraries in the acronym *GLAM*). National and international associations dealing with libraries, traditional archives, audiovisual archives and museums have organized joint conferences and envisaged the possibility of common principles for cataloging and classifying their resources. The increasing digitalization of metadata, as well as of resources themselves as in digital libraries, has speeded up this process through the *convergence* of all document types towards the digital form (Rayward, 1998).

Despite this, the history and features of each particular collection also matter in determining the best way of organizing and indexing it. Books kept in libraries have certain material features which affect the way they are sorted. The shape of books means that they can be arranged in linear sequences with only their spines showing, on which is printed their title and onto which a small label with a shelfmark can be pasted. Library classifications have exploited this feature to represent subjects by means of alphanumerical notations and arrange them in meaningful sequences. However, this solution can represent affinity between subjects along only a single dimension, while other affinity relationships that are orthogonal to these are lost (although faceted classifications mitigate this problem, see section 3.5.2). Also, outsize books may be grouped together for practical reasons, irrespective of their subject content.

In archives, unique documents are collected mainly depending on the institutional or private sources which have produced them. A common principle for their organization is the hierarchy of institutional departments and offices. This aspect, as codified in the principle of *provenance* (Tognoli and Guimarães, 2018), is usually the most important in archives. The subject content is often considered to be of lesser importance in archival metadata, although it can potentially be very useful. A police report kept in a local archive concerned a brawl at a rural feast and the sanctions imposed on those involved in it, but also included the minutes of a musician's examination, from which ethnomusicologists were able to discover relevant information about the existence at that place and time of a bagpipe. Similar situations can occur with paintings and frescos, documentary movies or even fictional movies that include interesting details in their settings.

It would be very useful to index these kinds of content, but also demanding, as every detail in a report or a scene could be relevant someday, and hence worth recording. This kind of indexing should focus on objects and events (that is, on phenomena) rather than on abstract categories. What is common to such different collections as libraries, archives and museums – despite the differences in the material shape and arrangement of their resources – is their objects, which ideally should be recorded in common indexes (Gnoli, 2010). The material features of documents and collections can be specified as further, separate components.

Museums and temporary expositions are collections of objects that document classes of natural phenomena – e.g. minerals, meteorites – or of human creations – e.g. archaeological remains, sculptures, paintings; collections of paintings are often called galleries. A similar function is performed by zoological and botanical gardens, which show living specimens as samples of their corresponding classes of organism: this makes the specimens another type of document (see section 1.3.1).

These items of knowledge content are in need of organization just as much as the contents of books or institutional records, but the method of doing so is clearly affected by their different nature, which ultimately is the only reason why they are kept in a museum or gallery rather than a library or archive (Kyle, 1959). Further, the full skeleton of a dinosaur may need a whole room, for practical reasons, while information on dinosaurs may also be contained in the remains of teeth shown in a separate showcase, as well as in a schema of paleontological eras on a poster nearby.

The disciplines of library science, archival science and museology all deal with the practical aspects of managing and organizing their particular kinds of collections. This dimension clearly is another relevant component in the organization of their contents. Some have emphasized how the particular choice of items in a collection, as well as the particular way of organizing them – which can be different from the organization of the same items in another collection – adds an 'authorial' component to KO, which may express the particular interests and personality of their curators, particularly in the case of private collections (Feinberg, 2011).

2.4.3 Documental approaches

Collections consist of *documents*, such as inscriptions, books, movies, websites, remains, specimens, etc. While books kept in libraries are the most classic type of document, they are by no means the only type, especially when we consider the various kinds of collections discussed in the previous section.

Robert Pagès (1948) suggested that anything can be a document insofar as it is used as such, that is, inasmuch as it conveys some knowledge. As an example, his teacher Suzanne Briet (1951) famously cited a live antelope, which is not a document when freely running in the wild, but becomes one when it is kept in a zoo to convey knowledge about antelopes in general. Pagès and Briet's pioneering approach is acknowledged by the contemporary leading expert in document theory Michael Buckland (2018). While agreeing that anything can in principle become a document, Buckland also acknowledges the important difference between documents that are originally created to be documents, like books, and documents that only secondarily become so, like the antelope.

> It is reasonable to consider any object that has documentary characteristics as a document; but, of course, that does not mean that it should be considered always and only in this way. A leek is not always and only an emblem of Welshness. The same is true in reverse: even an archetypal document, a printed book, can make a convenient doorstop, a role that depends on its physicality, not on any documentary aspect.
>
> (Buckland, 2018, 185)

Of course, specific kinds of documents have special characteristics that affect the way knowledge is treated in or through them. While a book will include just text and figures, a *Wikipedia* entry may also include audio recordings and moving images that help users to understand its content, such as the pronunciation of a sound or the dynamic transformation of a geometrical shape corresponding to a certain equation. Texts themselves are structured conventionally into paragraphs of certain lengths, for which papyrus rolls, codex books or web pages offer different possibilities for visualization and browsing.

These and other constraints lead authors to organize knowledge in their works into hierarchical units, like the volumes, chapters and sections of a monograph, each with a different title. These choices are ways to organize knowledge contents. More compact text forms, like articles, are collected by editors into a journal or a miscellaneous volume according to their general subject area, although each text may concern different aspects and details of the subject. Shorter text types are newspaper articles and blog posts, and even shorter ones are tweets or text (SMS) messages. In this series knowledge is increasingly fragmented – until being disaggregated into simple information (cf. section 1.1) – and in need of reconnection to broader frameworks through the active thought of its users. At the opposite end of this spectrum, large treatises and encyclopedias offer highly organized knowledge, the production of which has integrated a large number of other sources and research experience. Further factors that belong to the document dimension are the materials and production techniques: paper, ink, print, bindings of books, or the corresponding material components of other document types.

The study of these aspects of texts is carried out in the field of bibliology; other document types are studied by archaeology, epigraphy, numismatics, film studies, etc. On the other hand, the field called *documentation* since the pioneering treatise of Paul Otlet (1934) and the more recent *information science* (Bawden and Robinson, 2012) are more oriented towards the contents of documents. As they have a special historical connection to library science, they are also included in *library and information science*, shortened as *LIS* (Hjørland, 2017c). LIS deals with both the features of documents themselves and their accumulation, description, retrieval and use.

Most contemporary authors on KO consider themselves as belonging to the broader discipline of LIS because during the past century KO has developed mostly within LIS studies, as we saw in section 1.4. However, while LIS focuses on the documental dimension of knowledge, KO also covers the ways in which knowledge is categorized as part of the culture of a civilization, including its science, education, society and politics; for example, which subjects are taught in schools or dealt with in public offices and which are not, or how are they connected (why, for example, at the beginning of a curriculum in engineering it is mandatory to study some mathematics and physics, but not some history). Considering these aspects, we can better model the relationship between KO and LIS as one of intersection: there are parts of KO that are not LIS, such as school curricula or the history of concepts; and there are parts of LIS that are not KO, such as document loan regulations or library staff management.

The document dimension may be represented in KOSs by special terms or symbols to express that a subject is contained in a manual, a dictionary or a journal article, that it is recorded in a given document type (book, movie, specimen, etc.), a given form (text only, illustrations, audio, etc.) and a given format (printed, PDF, MP3, etc.). Some approaches to KO even take this dimension as primary and organize knowledge according to the documents in which it is contained.

This is the case with bibliometric approaches, which use statistics on large numbers of documents as a means to evaluate the intellectual production of recorded knowledge overall. KO aspects of this include such questions as which subjects are the most widespread, how their frequency changes over time, which other subject fields the most-cited documents belong to, and so on. Since 2014, a series of conferences on 'bibliometric-enhanced information retrieval' has been integrating such statistical data into search tools so that, for example, the results of a search include, besides documents that exactly match the query parameters, additional ones that are associated on the basis of a network of citation relationships.

Such relationships may include document metadata, such as a range of publication dates or the presence of a specific co-author, but also more sophisticated information such as citations of a document by others. Indeed citation networks, especially in digital media, are one important way in which clusters of related documents can be identified and proposed to users (Mayr and Scharnhorst, 2015).

Even the more traditional KOSs, such as classification schemes and subject heading lists, are partly determined by the document dimension. An important case is the old principle of *literary warrant* (Hulme, 1911; Barité, 2018), prescribing that only subjects that are actually dealt with in published documents should be included in a KOS. For example, if no book has yet been published about the molecular biology of businessmen, then a KOS should not include a class for this, despite it being a theoretically possible subject. A corollary of this principle is that KOSs tend to be developed in greater detail for domains where a significant number of documents have been published and are collected in libraries, archives or museums, while nobody spends any effort in constructing very detailed subclasses and facets for subjects that are hardly touched upon in the collected documentation.

As we shall see in section 2.4.5, this approach is quite different from the ontological one, which suggests developing KOSs according to the classes of known existing things, irrespective of whether they have already been discussed in the available sources. Indeed, displaying a certain little-investigated subject or allowing for a certain new combination of subjects in a KOS could be a stimulus to develop research on them and their potentially new connections (Swanson, 1986; Szostak et al., 2016, 14–18). If KO does not limit itself to existing documents, but focuses on knowledge contents itself, it can play a more active and creative role in the development of new knowledge.

2.4.4 Perspective approaches

Documents record and convey knowledge. However, knowledge is not as simple as the direct representation of individual phenomena. Rather, the way phenomena are connected, described and presented also depends very much on the particular perspective taken by the authors, editors and other creators of the documents. Although the ideal aim of knowledge seekers is to take 'a view from nowhere', as philosopher Thomas Nagel (1986) expressed it, in practice being completely neutral is not possible. Indeed, everybody is biased, more or less consciously, by their own particular background, context, purposes and so on.

We will call *perspective* the complex of these factors that affect the way knowledge is treated by every creator in every particular occasion. The philosophical branch dealing with how we acquire and develop our knowledge is *epistemology* (especially focusing on scientific knowledge, but often considered as a quasi-synonym of the more general *gnoseology*).

Foucault (1972) proposed the idea of an 'archaeology of knowledge', studying how different cultural epochs have treated certain subjects, especially such critical ones as mental illness or hospitalization. The very nature of disciplines is not neutral, as they are themselves the products of particular cultural processes: in order to study ethnobotany (the ways plants are known by people in different regions) a university classmate of mine had to travel to India, as he could not find this field in the curriculum of our natural sciences degree, which included only Western phytogeography (the distribution and association of plants in specific regions). He was facing a problem of perspective in KO!

Ignoring the perspective dimension of knowledge (γ) would mean naively assuming that a particular treatment of a topic is already its faithful, true and ultimate description. This was an attitude of positivism, a philosophical movement that flourished in the 19th century which elevated the knowledge abilities of humans, and the resulting sciences and technologies. Of course, these are good values in themselves, especially as opposed to superstition, fear and pessimistic skepticism. We all know that scientific knowledge has contributed enormously to improving the quality of life and intellectual achievements of mankind.

The excesses of presumption and trust observed in the positivistic, modernistic period have triggered a long-term reaction in intellectual environments that have developed into our *postmodern* period. Postmodernism emphasizes the relativity of knowledge manifestations, especially as knowledge is no longer seen as an exclusive product of Western culture. Globalization of exchanges has shown how the same topics can be seen in different ways by different peoples, just as they are by different social classes, genders, etc.

A classic example of these issues is the structure of the so-called 'universal' bibliographic classification systems developed since the end of the 19th century by American and English librarians, such as the Dewey Decimal Classification (DDC) or the Library of Congress Classification (LCC). While they have been important advances in KO – thanks to their technical features that will be examined in the following chapters (see especially section 4.4.5) – and are still very useful in libraries around the world, a critical analysis of them has revealed many biases due to the particular Western perspective of their creators.

In DDC one of the ten main classes (*200*) is devoted to religion: it is subdivided into ten subclasses, of which nine are for Christian religion and only the last one (*290*) is for all other religions! This could be reasonable in the context of Melvil Dewey's library, that of Amherst College in New York in 1876, if one considers the previously mentioned principle of literary warrant: it probably owned only a small number of books on Hinduism, Buddhism and Islam, although this of itself does not imply that these religions are less important than Christianity (in the first two cases, they are even much older). Thus, editors of other classification systems, like the DDC-derived UDC, have developed different orders of religion, which try to be more balanced, by allocating one subclass per major religion and listing these in historical order (Broughton, 2000). For similar reasons, the KOSs of Far Eastern countries that have been inspired by DDC, such as the Korean Decimal Classification and the Nippon Decimal Classification, need subdivisions different from those of the Western DDC. For example, calligraphy is a major class, as it is in Korean education, rather than being relegated to a deep subdivision (Kwasnik and Rubin, 2003; Choi, 2017).

Other examples can be found in LCC, which has a main class for 'military science' and another for 'naval science' (*U* and *V*, respectively). These are clearly of little use to many users, such as those of a Swiss library! In this case, as is implied by the name of the system, the scheme takes its structure from its original aim of organizing the collections of the Library of Congress, a major institutional facility in Washington, DC: the collection dimension has thus played a preeminent role, before LCC spread widely beyond the USA as a consequence of the Library's practice of sharing its bibliographic records with other interested libraries. Political analysts might comment that this is another way in which American culture is propagating its intellectual dominance in the contemporary world – but this is how things play out.

A large movement of *critical librarianship* is now developing in North America, encouraging librarians and users to 'decolonize' KO and LIS in general (La Barre, 2017). For example, more attention is being paid to Northern American or Oceanian native indigenous cultures, which can develop their own KOSs, such as the Brian Deer Classification, to more accurately express their way of organizing knowledge (Doyle and Metoyer, 2015).

A pioneer in the critical analysis of KOSs is Hope A. Olson, especially with her book meaningfully titled *The Power to Name* (Olson, 2002), showing that biases towards dominant classes are often hidden in subject headings and other KOSs. Discriminated minorities often include women, who should be better served by specific gender studies (López-Huertas, 2013), or gay people (Campbell, 2004), or migrants of various ethnic origins. In the past decade, there has been a debate, involving many American librarians, about the subject heading *illegal aliens*, which was found to be offensive towards foreign persons cited in documents on migration and was removed from the Library of Congress Subject Headings (LCSH) (although removing it from all library catalogs that apply LCSH will take a much longer time).

Knowledge perspectives change not only across space but also across time. A concept developed in the culture of a certain epoch may change slowly over the years, as can the meaning of a corresponding label in a KOS. This evolution has been described as *subject ontogeny* (Tennis, 2002). Due to such processes it is no trivial matter to understand the exact meaning, for example, of *patritius* in ancient Roman sociology, or *feud* in medieval law, nor should these terms and concepts be applied to different epochs without care (Bloch, 1952).

All these issues can be summarized in Clare Beghtol's notion of *cultural warrant*, which covers a variety of related ideas such as 'viewpoint warrant' and should complement that of literary warrant, discussed in section 2.4.3. In other words, KOSs should enable their users to represent the different cultural perspectives of documents and their authors, not just a dominant one (Beghtol, 2002).

The perspectives according to which knowledge is presented also depend on general philosophical attitudes. Hjørland (2017a, sect. 4.2c) has identified four major philosophical approaches in KO and LIS. Despite his tendency to present them as alternatives, others have found that several of them can be used together in an 'eclectic' development of KOSs (Dousa and Ibekwe-San Juan, 2014). The four approaches are:

- the *rationalist* approach, assuming that knowledge and its organization can start from the human faculty of reason, which can impose an a priori order on topics, as envisaged by the 17th-century philosophers Descartes, Spinoza and Leibniz. This operates when, for example, categories are identified according to a top-down process of logical division (Frické, 2016) which splits general concepts into more specific ones, as in the hierarchy of Porphyry's Tree (see section 1.4.2); or when abstract categories like those of Aristotle are applied to define concepts analytically (a 'human' is a rational animal; a 'girl' is a female young human; etc.), as in Dahlberg's (1978) theory of concepts;
- the *empiricist* approach, emphasizing that knowledge, rather than being assumed in abstract ways, should come through observation and experience, as the philosophers Locke, Hobbes and Hume have argued. For example, the biological school of 'phenetic' or 'numerical taxonomy' has argued that organisms should be classified on the basis of as many empirical characters as possible, without prior reference to any particular theory concerning their relativeness (Gnoli, 2018a);
- the *hermeneutical* or *historical* approach, which considers the development of knowledge schools and their contents in their original contexts, as recommended by various postmodern philosophers. This operates in Foucault's archaeology of knowledge and much contemporary academic research in KO;
- the *pragmatic* approach, which emphasizes the applications for which knowledge has been conceived and developed, claiming that they cannot be separated from its contents, as inspired by the pragmatist school of philosophers John Dewey, William James and others. For example, Vickery (2008) has suggested that, together with the phenomena studied, such as stars or plants, KOSs should also be based on the 'activities' for which people need and develop knowledge, such as agriculture, medicine or amusement. Pragmatism is often combined with the hermeneutical approach, a choice adopted by Hjørland, who describes himself as a 'pragmatic realist': although knowledge is indeed about an existing reality out there, it is always compenetrated with historical and pragmatic factors that have to be taken into account. Hjørland's view thus revives librarian

Jesse Shera's *social epistemology* (Egan and Shera, 1952), having argued that knowledge, and libraries curating it, are primarily social actors.

These two approaches – hermeneutical and pragmatic – are joined in the largely influential KO paradigm of *domain analysis* (Hjørland, 2017b). According to this, KO should be studied by first considering the discourse communities that have developed certain intellectual schemes, categories and terminologies, as these are an expression of their pragmatic purposes. For example, academics who develop a particular domain in a particular time and place context will categorize their knowledge differently from academics of different traditions, or laypeople informed only by the mass media, or indigenous peoples living in countries away from Western civilization. Domain analysis thus argues that the perspective dimension (γ) is necessarily compenetrated with the social one (η), while the universality of human knowledge faculties (θ), which is emphasized in user-based approaches (see section 2.4.1), will be largely over-rated (Hjørland, 2013).

All this would imply that calling general classification systems like DDC or LCC 'universal', as was common in the 20th century, is illusory. The idea of universality was debated at an ASIS&T workshop (Tennis, 2014) where various speakers agreed with the positions described above. On the other hand, Rick Szostak and I have argued that while universality should not be viewed in the positivistic sense of ultimate truth, it is still required by the practical need of sharing knowledge between different authors, peoples and perspectives – that is, for conceptual interoperability. While we know that translation from one language or a KOS to another can never be perfect, as each one is biased by a complex network of cultural perspectives, every time one KOS is mapped to another one in order to connect different resources (as in linked open data techniques), some universality has to be assumed. People with different backgrounds can lose much through translation, but still can communicate in some way.

In order to enable interdisciplinary and intercultural communication, Szostak (2008) has proposed that the different theories and methods that can be adopted in documents should be listed in special tables, then combined with the phenomena studied in a synthetic classification. In every discipline, e.g. economics, different theoretical approaches exist, e.g. classical capitalism, Marxism, neoliberalism, etc., that can be represented as separate subjects. Identifying the particular theory adopted in a document may not always be trivial, especially in fields such as politics or philosophy, where theories are more entangled and fuzzier – but indexers can attempt to represent them. Methods, such as interviews, statistics or laboratory analysis, are usually less numerous and are more easily identified and represented.

2.4.5 Phenomenon approaches

In Szostak's proposal the representation of theories and methods, that is, the perspective dimension, can be combined with that of phenomena (β) by the techniques of analytico-synthetic classification, which will be illustrated in section 3.5. For example, a document may be indexed as being about 'rosaceae [phenomenon], studied by phenetic taxonomy [theory], by DNA analysis [method]'. This framework has been summarized in the León Manifesto (ISKO Italia, 2007), subscribed by various KO researchers after an ISKO Spain conference on interdisciplinarity and transdisciplinarity held in the town of León.

Interdisciplinarity is indeed another important requirement in KO (Szostak et al., 2016). Traditional disciplines, such as philosophy, medicine or literature, are a result of the development of knowledge in past centuries, especially in the universities. Disciplines and domains belong to the perspective dimension, as the same subject can be treated differently depending on the disciplinary approach of the authors. Indeed, disciplines have often been listed according to the epistemological distinction between three main faculties of human knowledge: the sciences of reason, such as philosophy and pure sciences; those of imagination, such as literature and the arts; and those of memory, such as geography and history. As we saw in section 1.4.5, this tripartition originates from Francis Bacon and came through various authors until DDC and UDC, which still follow a basically epistemological order.

On the other hand, contemporary knowledge is increasingly interdisciplinary, and connections between different disciplines are often encouraged as they tend to produce fruitful contaminations, like the application of an idea from one discipline to another one. A major case was naturalist Charles Darwin's reading of Thomas Malthus's economics essay on the struggle for limited resources, which inspired him to apply the same idea to the biological domain of variability in natural populations, thus originating his revolutionary theory of evolution by natural selection.

In order to benefit from useful ideas in domains other than their own, researchers should be able to search for a particular phenomenon or a particular theory or method irrespective of disciplinary boundaries, as recommended by Szostak. However, as various KO researchers have observed (Jacob, 1994; Beghtol, 1998), the classification systems adopted in most libraries and databases are still based on disciplines – even worse, on disciplines as they were listed 150 years ago.

More recent KOSs, like thesauri and ontologies, list concepts and terms more freely, so they can represent either phenomena, like *rosaceae*, or perspectives, like *phenetic taxonomy*. However, these KOSs usually represent only the relationships of concepts and terms to closely related ones, rather than offering general frameworks of knowledge as traditional classifications do. Another type of KOS are scientific taxonomies, such as those of plants, animals or languages, which also list phenomena rather than perspectives. However, scientific taxonomies are only indirectly used to index documents, as parts of them are incorporated into bibliographic classifications (DDC class *590* 'zoology' is divided according to zoological taxonomy).

This suggests that there is a need for KOSs that represent a general order of concepts, although independently from traditional disciplines. Such *phenomenon-based classifications* have indeed been proposed since early 20th century, in James Duff Brown's Subject Classification, which allowed for indexing documents by 'concrete subject' followed by the particular standpoint (perspective) under which it is studied (Beghtol, 2004).

The idea of listing phenomena instead of disciplines was especially studied in the 1960s by members of the CRG such as Douglas Foskett and Derek Austin, who drafted a new general scheme of this kind for a project sponsored by NATO (Austin, 1969). Unfortunately the project ended before a finalized classification could be produced, although Austin reused some important ideas to develop a verbal indexing system, PRECIS, used in the British National Bibliography. More recently, CRG's ideas have been resumed in the Integrative Levels Classification (ILC) research project, which is developing a new phenomenon-based classification, also allowing the expression of perspective, document, etc., although these are subordinated to phenomena (Gnoli, 2016). A similar project has been proposed by Szostak with his Basic Concepts Classification.

As ILC notation is also capable of expressing other structural features of KOSs that will be dealt with in the next chapter, such as systematic order, hierarchies, facets and themes, we will use it to provide examples of these, although our treatment for the general purposes of this book will not be committed to any single KOS.

If one abandons the traditional epistemological orders originating from Bacon, which other principles can one adopt to structure phenomenon-based systems?

The kinds of phenomena, that is, the objects of knowledge, are studied by the philosophical branch of *ontology*, literally 'the discourse on what exists'. Ontology (not to be confused with digital ontologies, which are a type of KOS applying certain ontological principles to represent concepts and their relationships) deals with such categories as entities, attributes, processes, or wholes, parts, individuals, which can be used to organize concepts in general systems (Poli, 1996). We will find some of these categories again when discussing facet analysis, a major structural technique in KO (see section 3.5.1).

One ontological theory that has been found to be useful by various KO authors is general systems theory, developed in the mid-20th century by Ludwig von Bertalanffy, Kenneth Boulding and others. This theory introduces the notion of a generic *system*, that is, any structure organized into parts and functions, as can be found in nature – think of a galaxy or a cell – as well as in society and human products – think of a school, a government or a car. In all these examples it is always possible to consider the whole system as well as its parts and the relationships between them. General systems theory thus allows one to model any kind of phenomena and to represent their internal and external connections and relationships, e.g. by facets. Its use in LIS has especially been considered by Foskett (1972) and applied to PRECIS by Austin.

Another ontological theory that has been repeatedly applied in KO is that of levels of reality, especially developed by Nicolai Hartmann but also followed more or less explicitly by many other authors in different traditions, some of whom have called it the theory of 'integrative levels' (Poli, 2001; Kleineberg, 2017). This theory identifies a series of levels of increasing organization in the world, including those of forms (like mathematical and logical entities), matter (like quarks, atoms, molecules and rocks), life (like cells, organisms and populations), mind (like senses, emotions and reason), society (like communities, governments and economies) and cultural heritage (like material, artistic and intellectual products of human activity). We have already met ontical levels in section 1.1.2 when speaking of informational systems (genes, brains, languages, documents) at various levels.

This series offers an obvious sequence in which major classes in a KOS can be listed, as well as sequences for their subclasses (e.g. a sequence of biological classes can be genes, prokaryote organisms, eukaryote organisms, populations, species, ecosystems; and eukaryotes can be further divided into algae, fungi, plants, animals). Several bibliographic classifications have followed it, including disciplinary ones like the Bliss Bibliographic Classification, where disciplines are sorted according to the level of the phenomena they study. Levels are an even more obvious criterion for phenomenon-based systems, such as Brown's Subject Classification, CRG's draft system or ILC.

With ontological approaches, we have now completed the review of the dimensions that can be taken into account in KO theories (as dimension of reality in itself cannot be directly attained in formal expressions of knowledge). Every dimension – cognition, people, information needs, collections, documents, perspectives, and phenomena – is worth being considered and can contribute to the theory of KO. Different studies and different systems may give more relevance to one or another of these. We now move to consider the structural principles on which KO systems can be based.

CHAPTER 3

Structural principles in knowledge organization

3.1 Words in natural language

As mentioned in section 2.2, concepts are the basic units of KO. Concepts classify the variety of experience in individual notions, which can be related to other concepts in information networks. However, concepts are not material entities. In order to be shared and transmitted in a culture through its media, either oral or recorded, they need to be expressed in some way.

The most common way to express concepts is by words; other symbols, like gestures, icons or any shared code, can also work. In a sense, then, words in natural languages are a basic form of KO: when we say *that cat*, we are classing the phenomenon we observe as an instance of the class of cats.

Words are listed in dictionaries with a definition that describes their meaning. *Cat* means 'a small carnivoran mammal with tail ...', etc. Such definitions are intended to enumerate the *essential characteristics* of a class, according to the classical philosophy of language, which refers to Aristotle's logic. Essential characteristics, such as being a mammal or having a tail, are opposed to accidental ones, such as having an injured nose or enjoying pasta, which may occur but are not necessary in order to be classed as a member of cats.

However, even supposedly essential characteristics may occasionally be missing: a breed of cat from the Isle of Man is tailless. This has led some language psychologists, especially Eleanor Rosch, to argue that classes refer only to *prototypes*: although the prototypical cat has a tail, certain tailless animals can still be called cats, as they have several other characteristics of the class.

Because many documents are in the form of written texts, their words and phrases can be a starting point for KO. Nowadays words are usually recorded in a digital format, either originally or after a digitalization procedure by optical character recognition. The full text of a document can then be scanned by a search engine for any particular word or combination of words that a user is interested in. Document editors may have emphasized certain words by writing them in italic or bold type, or by putting them in the title, section headings, abstract or keyword list, and searching can exploit this by assuming that these words are especially relevant in that document.

(Obviously, this approach does not work for knowledge sources that are not expressed in written words, such as images or audiovisual documents. However, they may be provided with captions or other textual metadata that describe them, and these can be searched in the usual ways. Alternatively, special algorithms may scan the document and identify shapes, colors, sounds or other relevant elements in it. See section 6.3.4 for multimedia information retrieval.)

Advanced algorithms can also be applied to the full text using techniques of *natural language processing* (*NLP*): word indexes are generated automatically, from which common and usually irrelevant words (*stopwords*) are removed; rarely occurring words, such as names, are considered to be of special relevance; the frequency of each word is calculated, and so on.

Operating on a statistical basis, algorithms can associate a document with a *cluster* of documents with similar statistical values, e.g. where the words *grape, vine, vineyard, viticulture, wine, wine-making* occur with a greater frequency than in average documents. There is a high probability that these documents will belong to a specific domain – although not certainly, as accidental factors may affect the calculations (e.g. *Wine* can occur as a personal name not related to actual wine).

While clustering is a crude NPL technique, results can be refined by using it in conjunction with other information sources. Words can be matched with a dictionary listing relevant and non-relevant words. Words can also be compared with those in a KOS, such as a thesaurus (see section 4.4.4), which provides additional information on relationships with other terms: as *viticulture* is known to be subordinated to the broader term *agriculture*, the algorithm may conclude that the document belongs to the domain of agriculture. Of special efficiency is the provision of a set of 'training' documents in the same domain that have previously been classified by humans: algorithms can statistically compare the known documents with the new ones to decide whether they belong to the same class or not.

We will discuss word-based techniques for automatic subject indexing of texts (Golub, 2017) in section 6.3.3. For now, we will continue with reviewing the basic structures in KO, and look at a further step in their sophistication.

3.2 Terms in controlled vocabularies

While natural languages are themselves a rudimentary form of KO, their efficiency in this respect is by no means optimal. This is because natural languages are the result of complex historical processes that have been affected by many factors, rather than being designed in a rational way to serve retrieval purposes. Their grammars are often irregular, with weird exceptions that have to be learned by speakers, not suitable to be treated in formal ways. Meaning is something fuzzy, especially for words that can occur in many different contexts, such as *right, bad, management* or *freedom.* Thus, natural language can serve only as a first approximation in the technical treatment of knowledge.

In order to be useful for KO, language has to be modified so as to acquire the traits of regularity and predictability that are needed in formal tools. It has to become an *indexing language* (Hutchins, 1975) or *documentary language* – that is, a special artificial language conceived for the purposes of indexing and documentation. These terms were especially common in earlier decades as awareness of the linguistic properties that are relevant to information science increased; today they have been largely replaced by the similar notion of *knowledge organization system,* which places more emphasis on their structure and function (see section 4.1).

Another related term is *controlled vocabulary,* which is often used as a quasi-synonym of *KOS,* although it more properly refers to an important subset of KOSs, those consisting of words (hence excluding classifications) that are formally controlled (hence excluding keywords and folksonomies; see section 4.4).

Still, the term *controlled vocabulary* is expressive of a core part of KO procedures: those that enable moving from the vocabulary of a natural language to the more formal and powerful terms of a subject headings list or a thesaurus. We will discuss such procedures in this section.

The basic idea of controlled vocabularies is that each concept should be expressed by one and only one controlled word, rather than in various and fuzzy ways as can be done (even on purpose, for stylistic or poetical reasons) in natural language. Once a word has been controlled and selected to be part of a KOS, it becomes a *term.* A term may consist of either one or several words as they correspond to an individual concept. Such terms as *health care, washing machines* or *knowledge organization* indeed consist of several words although expressing a single concept.

A first problem in many natural languages, including the European ones in which most international literature is currently written, is that words change according to grammar. *Care* may be either a noun or a verb; as a noun, it can be found in the plural form *cares;* as a verb, it can change according to person (*he cares*), tense (*cared*), etc. How can formal procedures identify all these forms as one and the same concept?

The solution that has spread in KO since the 20th century is to standardize the grammatical forms according to stable rules. In indexes – for example, in a subject headings list (see section 4.4.3) – words should always be in the form of nouns (*care, management*) rather than the corresponding verbs (*to care, to manage*). If a verb has no corresponding noun, it can be nominalized by its gerundive form (*drinking*). These rules lump all occurrences of a word under one and the same term in the list. In automatic indexing, algorithms may be instructed to identify grammatical endings according to the rules of a particular language (e.g. *-s*, *-ed*, *-ing* for English) and to routinely lump their occurrences into a single set.

A similar rule concerns plurals. While some words (*sheep*) are not countable, many others change their endings in the plural forms (*cat/cats*). In most controlled vocabularies, the rule is that the plural form (*cats*) should be adopted when available. This choice also expresses the fact that a term usually expresses a class (all existing cats) rather than an individual (this particular cat), as documents tend to refer to general knowledge about them rather than anecdotal information; even a newspaper story involving a particular cat is often interesting to most readers only as a case of what can happen with cats, rather than for that individual (the latter information will be relevant mainly to the cat's owners, who are already informed, before the newspaper is produced).

Besides morphological control, another major issue is lexical control. Natural languages often use different words to express the same concept, which is clearly not functional for the purposes of KO because it scatters the concept under several headings. *Automobiles*, *cars* and *motor cars* may refer to the same phenomenon in different knowledge sources according to local usage or to English vs. American usage. In KO, one form must be chosen as the *preferred term*, and the others will be recorded as its synonyms:

> cars
> > UF *automobiles, motor-cars*
> *automobiles*, USE *cars*
> *motor-cars*, USE *cars.*

UF (used for) and *USE* are standard markers of lexical relationships in thesauri. Subject heading lists often adopt *See* instead of *USE* to perform basically the same function – that is, to direct to a preferred term in the KOS. A user looking for a non-preferred term will thus be directed to the preferred term and will be able to launch a search for that term. Provided that indexing has been performed carefully, this will yield all occurrences of the concept in the knowledge base to hand.

The same situation as with lexical synonyms can also occur with common vs. scientific nouns, or with full vs. abbreviated forms of a complex term. These can be handled by the same kind of cross-reference:

> *AIDS*, USE *acquired immune deficiency syndrome*
> *KO*, USE *knowledge organization*
> *PDE*, USE *partial differential equations*
> *vulpes*, USE *foxes.*

Some systems also include cross-references from quasi-synonyms (terms with a very close though not identical meaning, like *warm dishes, See hot dishes*), from antonyms (opposite terms, like *cold dishes, See hot dishes*) or for names of disciplines that study the corresponding objects (*ornithology, See birds*). Their purpose is always to make indexing of and searching for these concepts more consistent.

Terms are studied in terminology, a branch across linguistics and information science. Terminology is especially relevant in very specific domains that have developed special terms used in academic language but not known by laypeople, like *diagenesis* in geology or *synapomorphy* in systematic biology. While they may be listed in domain glossaries, they may not always be found in general dictionaries.

Proper names are sometimes excluded from controlled vocabularies but may be listed in special KOSs such as gazetteers, that is, lists of geographical names. Dictionaries, glossaries and gazetteers are simple examples of KOSs, mainly consisting in ordered lists. We will now consider how terms can be listed.

3.3 Lists

Lists are a simple and early way of organizing concepts, as we saw in section 1.4.1. Words or terms identifying concepts are simply juxtaposed one after the other, so that they can be browsed, compared or counted. A series of entries listed together in a KOS is also known as an *array*, as in Ranganathan's (1967) terminology for classification systems and in computer programming languages.

Arrays are sets of terms, like {*plants, red algae, animals, fungi*}. In this example they are in no particular order, that is, they are an unordered set (cf. section 1.2). Order may not be very important, so long as the list includes only few entries, as users can quickly read them all and find the relevant one. However, we know that most users are willing to browse a list of only a few tens of entries (their futility point, see section 2.4.1) before giving up. This means that as the list becomes longer there is a need for some principle by which entries are ordered. In ordered lists users (including machines) know a structuring principle and exploit it to jump quickly to the relevant section of the list, without having to browse through the entries.

Various ordering principles are known, both conventional and conceptual. Ranganathan (1967, 183–97) identified and discussed eight basic principles for producing a 'helpful sequence' in a classification system, which are still largely viable in contemporary KO. These are 'alphabetical sequence, literary warrant, canonical sequence, increasing complexity, quantitative measure, spatial contiguity, later-in-evolution, later-in-time'. We will review them in the following subsections.

3.3.1 Alphabetical vs. systematic order

The most common conventional principle follows alphabetical order, that is, the traditional sequence of written letters (*a, b, c, ... z*) (Korwin and Lund, 2019). An unordered list can thus become an ordered list: (*animals, fungi, plants, red algae*).

A big advantage of alphabetical order is that it is well known to users. Most letters and their position in the order are common to all languages that use the Roman alphabet. Languages that use different writing systems, such as Greek, Russian or Chinese, obviously follow different orders. Today, however, even those writing systems have transliteration rules that enable the representation of their words in the Roman alphabet, so that only one additional alphabet – the Roman one – is needed besides that of the user's mother tongue.

The only writing system used more widely than the Roman alphabet is the Hindu–Arabic numerals (*0, 1, ... 9*), which are used in the notation of many international classifications. The Hindu–Arabic numerals and the Roman alphabet are also used routinely by computers (in the form of the ASCII and Unicode standards) for sorting functions, hence they are eminently suited for processing terms and symbols for KO purposes.

The use of letters in natural-language words has no special connection to their meaning, as it depends on etymology. The distribution of terms in an alphabetical list may then be considered a random one, as we can observe by looking at any section of a dictionary: ... *potential, potentilla, pother, pot-house, potion, pot-pourri, pottage, potted*, ...

This means that in alphabetical lists, while a term can be found in a predictable position for scanning purposes, it will have no special relationship with the neighboring terms, and the overall list will be mixed. This is the opposite of the general purposes of KO. That is why Ranganathan listed alphabetical sequence as the last resort among his principles for helpful sequence (they are cited above in his reverse order of priority): he was much more interested in more powerful principles.

The alternative to alphabetical order can be called systematic or conceptual order – that is, a sequence depending on the meaning of terms rather than on their surface form. For example, most handbooks of systematic biology will list the four classes of our previous example in this sequence:

> *fungi*
> *red algae*
> *plants*
> *animals.*

Due to the accidents of etymology, however, this sequence cannot be reproduced automatically if the entries are mixed and then sorted again. Indeed, automatic procedures are usually available to produce only alphabetical order. To solve this problem, we need to associate a special meaningful code, a notation, to each entry, in such a way that the alphabetical order of the codes corresponds to the desired order of our entries:

mn   fungi
mo   red algae
mp   plants
mq   animals.

Notation is a key feature in bibliographic classification schemes which can be used to control the ordering of books on shelves or of records in catalogs. It can consist of letters, numerals and punctuation marks. Letters and numerals must have a conventional order, like: (*0, 1, 2 ... 8, 9, A, B, C, ... Y, Z, a, b, c, ... y, z*), so they must be chosen in such a way as to produce a helpful systematic sequence of the classes they identify. In the example above the class of fungi is given a combination of letters (*mn*) which precedes those of the other classes so that it is listed before them in the systematic order, which is desirable according to a principle of evolution (see below).

Notation can also be used to express other structural principles, such as hierarchies (in our example it expresses the fact that all classes are part of the superclass *m* 'eukaryote organisms') or relationships with other classes (*mq4mn* means 'animals affected by fungi' in ILC). This will be seen in the coming examples as we will discuss the corresponding structural principles.

Let us now consider Ranganathan's principles for helpful sequences other than the alphabetical one, which can all be used to create a systematic order.

3.3.2 Literary warrant

This refers to Hulme's notion of classes for which some actual documents exist in a collection (see section 2.4.3). For example, eukaryote organisms also include living forms that have been discovered very recently, for which little documentation exists as yet, such as hemimastigophora. While they are discussed in some sections of zoological treatises, our target collection may not include any whole document on hemimastigophora. This may lead KOS developers not to create any class for them, but just to recommend classifying them under eukaryote organisms in general.

On the other hand, fungi, red algae, plants and animals will each probably be covered by several documents. Suppose that most biological books cover animals, followed by plants, fungi and red algae. We can then decide to list them in this order to reflect literary warrant:

    A   animals
    B   plants
    C   fungi
    D   red algae.

This principle is only slightly less arbitrary than that of alphabetization. Indeed, abundance of documentation does not necessarily correspond to any structural trait of the listed phenomena. While they may be less documented, red algae may share more with plants than with fungi (say, ability to photosynthesize), making their separation from plants in the list a bad idea. However, literary warrant may still be useful in some contexts. Think of a search engine displaying the results of a query on organisms. As most available websites deal with animals, it can make sense that resources on animals are displayed first, because (1) users will find more under this class than under other classes, (2) many users will probably be thinking of resources on animals rather than on red algae.

A related principle adopted in search engines is popularity: websites that have been visited more often by previous users may be displayed first, as it can be expected that they will also satisfy the new users. Of course, neither literary warrant nor popularity means that the corresponding resources are better than those on less popular topics, especially in a scientific context. The party most voted for is not necessarily the one most suitable to rule. If we are really passionate about the structure of our world, we will not be content with literary warrant alone.

3.3.3 Canonical sequence

Another systematic principle that still has a large conventional component is canonical sequence. This is the most obvious choice when one needs to list items that are traditionally listed in a certain sequence: in this case, adopting a different sequence would be confusing for users.

Canons are especially important in literature, philosophy and religion. The books included in the Bible are traditionally published in a certain sequence, which does not necessarily reflect the exact order in which they have been composed or other criteria (the Apocalypse is ordered last, despite being composed by the same author as St John's Gospel). Days of the week are listed in the well-known sequence by convention: both a KOS listing them in alphabetical order (*Friday, Monday* ...) and one listing them in chronological order starting with *Wednesday* would confuse users, because this would break the canonical sequence.

3.3.4 Increasing complexity

With this principle we move to consideration of some intrinsic characteristics of the ordered phenomena.

Complexity is a common guiding principle when illustrating the various aspects of a given subject one after the other: one starts with the simplest cases or elements, gradually adding more components. This chapter itself illustrates the structural principles of KO in order of increasing complexity, starting with words and lists as the simplest structures and continuing with increasingly complex structures; the next chapter will do the same with KOS types, starting from the simplest and proceeding to the most sophisticated.

Geometric figures are often studied in this sequence: teachers start with triangles, followed by quadrangles, then polygons with an increasing number of sides; within triangles, they start from equilateral ones, which are the most simple to describe and measure, and then proceed to isosceles and scalene ones, which have more complex properties. If one considers a hierarchy of specificity, the result will be somewhat contrary:

A	triangles	
AA	scalene triangles	
AB	isosceles triangles	
ABA		equilateral triangles

which would lead to studying the easiest subject only at the end of the sequence.

3.3.5 Quantitative measure

This is a very intuitive property of phenomena, although not often a very significant one. Whales and elephants are not necessarily more (or less) interesting than colibris and crickets. In some cases, however, priority by size is reasonable. To list cities, one may want to start with Tokyo and Mexico City rather than Swansea or Brive-la-Gaillarde.

3.3.6 Spatial contiguity

Speaking of geographical entities (McIlwaine, 2004), spatial contiguity is obviously an important alternative. It is usually adopted when listing countries or landscape features. The same principle is used when listing the planets by their increasing distance from the Sun rather than by their size or chemical composition. Rooms in a house, anatomical parts or components in an engine may follow the same general principle.

One tricky problem arises when two- or three-dimensional spaces are considered. In such cases, they do not offer any obvious linear sequence. For example, take a list of the states of the USA. We may decide to start conventionally from the north-west with Washington, but do we then proceed southwards with Oregon or eastwards with Idaho?

Ranganathan suggested starting from the center of a land (which can often be most relevant in a way) then to move north, north-east and so on, clockwise. The official numbering of arrondissements in Paris follows a similar principle: the *1er* is in the center, *2e* to *9e* form a circle around it, and *10e* to *18e* form a further, external circle; thus we automatically know that the *14e* (Montparnasse) will be quite peripheral and towards the south-west. (In case you are beginning to applaud French administration for its KO skills, you will change your mind after looking at the system of department codes, *01* to *99*: these just reflect the alphabetical order of department names and are therefore redundant information that does not add any useful detail; code *45* only tells you that the corresponding department name, Loiret, is around the middle of the alphabetical order!)

Another possibility for subdividing a territory is by watersheds, as these cover the whole surface and reflect such significant features as main valleys and rivers (although this is much less relevant in plains and dry regions). Furthermore, watersheds can be subdivided into their tributary sections. Verdin and Verdin (1999) illustrate a clever decimal notation to express proximity to river source vs. mouth and the hierarchy of tributaries.

3.3.7 Later-in-evolution

Evolution is a process occurring in many contexts. The most famous case is the evolution of organisms, well known in theoretical biology: some organisms, such as unicellular algae, have appeared at earlier evolutionary stages, while others, such as birds, are a more recent result of a long history. This offers an obvious principle for ordering them, from the most primitive to the most evolved. But practically all classes of phenomena also evolve: think of stars, soils, biomes, languages, cultures and so on.

Many special sciences have considered evolutionary principles by which to organize their objects, and terms for such taxonomies are various, including 'genetic', 'phylogenetic', 'genealogical', etc. (Gnoli, 2018a). Philosophers of science often consider a general, cosmological evolution from the simplest subatomic phenomena, through molecules and cells, to the most sophisticated creations of the human spirit. This inspires the general order of main classes in several systems (Dousa, 2009), including Brown's Subject Classification, Bliss Bibliographic Classification, Russian Library-Bibliographical Classification and the ILC. The evolutionary principle is often related with that of complexity (see section 3.3.4), but there are also cases, such as that of parasitic organisms, where the more evolved forms are simpler than their ancestors.

3.3.8 Later-in-time

Time can also be connected to evolutionary stages. Again, however, the correlation is not automatic: many present forms, like bacteria, are little evolved as compared to older ones, like dinosaurs; Sanskrit was a highly sophisticated language, but is no longer spoken. The world's history is more complex than a single progressive process in one direction. In this sense, time is a most general principle, as almost anything can be referred to a specific period when it has existed, including the formation of a galaxy, geological and paleontological eras, historical periods, centuries, years, seasons, etc. Ranganathan thus assigns the top position among his principles for helpful sequence to time.

However, there are entities, such as numbers or triangles, that do not exist in any particular time – suggesting to certain philosophers that they are eternal. Other principles, such as complexity (see 3.3.4), are thus needed to order them. It would seem that no single principle by itself is sufficient to order everything.

3.4 Hierarchies

While lists are a simple way to organize entities, they have a remarkable limitation: very long lists are not easy to use. If we were to list all phenomena in the world in one single list, that would consist of thousands or millions of entries (depending on how detailed our terminology is).

Admittedly, by applying a predictable principle such as alphabetical order or time, we can, in principle, scroll through the whole list quickly until we find the items we are interested in. However, this approach does not allow us to form a picture of the whole of available knowledge. Furthermore, in a flat list many relevant relationships between entries will be missed: *animals* and *plants* are filed in positions far apart, with no clue that they are related as both being multicellular organisms.

To manage this, all cultures have always split lists into more manageable chunks, thus producing groups of entities; that is, they have divided a single set of all concepts into several subsets.

Listing by some of the principles discussed above can now be applied within each group; and the groups themselves need to be listed by some principle – which can be either the same as is adopted within the groups or a different one. The principle can obviously be repeated as many times as needed, thus producing a hierarchical tree of classes.

'Trees' are an old metaphor, used to represent such conceptual structures since the time of Porphyry's Tree; the only illustration in Darwin's *Origin of Species* is a sketched evolutionary tree; and in contemporary graph theory the undirected graphs in which any two vertices are connected by a single path are called *trees*.

An important KOS type structured as hierarchical trees are thesauri (see section 4.4.4). Thesauri organize terms, which are connected by hierarchical relationships which take special names: for example, *flowering plants* has *plants* as a *broader term* (BT), and *monocotyledons* as a *narrower term* (NT):

flowering plants
  UF *angiosperms*
  BT *plants*
  NT *monocotyledons*
  ...

3.4.1 Types

In hierarchical trees every class can be divided into *subclasses*, these in turn into sub-subclasses and so on. Subclasses are more specific than classes, so that knowledge about the more general class includes that on its subclasses – claiming that plants do photosynthesis implies that ferns also do photosynthesis; claiming that animals breathe implies that insects also breathe:

fungi
red algae
plants
  ferns
  flowering plants
animals
  molluscs
  arthropods
    arachnids
    crustaceans
    insects.

In this example every subclass can be said to be a *type* or a *kind* of the more general class: arthropods are a type of animals, and insects are a type of arthropods. Traditional logic also calls arthropods a *genus* and insects its *species*. It states that species can be defined by the same properties as their genera, plus some *differentia specifica*, that is, some additional properties that identify insects but not, e.g., crustaceans. Notice that (unlike in biological terminology) *arthropods* in turn are a species of a more general genus, *animals*, which in turn are a species of *organisms* and so on. To avoid ambiguity of the term, we will simply talk about 'subclasses' or 'types'. The idea is that division into subclasses can be reiterated as many times as is needed.

Types are a very useful way of structuring knowledge, as they synthesize large amounts of information. The class of *animals* summarizes a complex set of properties that are owned by all animals. These also apply to all types of animals: for example, as all animals are made of cells, arthropods also are made of cells. Clearly, the opposite is not true: while arthropods are structured in a series of segments (metameres), not all animals are.

This can also be expressed by saying that as one moves from types down to their subtypes, sub-subtypes, etc., class intension increases: that is, the definition of arthropods implies more properties, like being structured in segments, than does the definition of animals. On the other hand, along the same series, class extension decreases: that is, *arthropods* refers to a more limited set of phenomena than *animals*: there are fewer arthropods than animals.

When using a notation to control the sorting of entries, each rank of subdivision is often expressed by an additional digit:

mq	animals	
mqn		molluscs
mqr		arthropods
mqrd		arachnids
mqrh		crustaceans
mqri		insects.

At each particular rank the notation controls the helpful sequence of classes: molluscs are listed before arthropods because they are considered to be less evolved than arthropods; within arthropods, crustaceans precede insects for a similar reason; and so on. Additional digits make subclasses, like *mqr*, to be listed immediately after their parent class (*mq*) and before their own subclasses (*mqrd*).

Ranks of subdivision are sometimes called 'levels', but we will not use this term because it produces confusion with levels of organization, as described in section 2.4.5. A useful terminology is that of Ranganathan, who calls any sequence of increasing specificity a *chain*, such as 'animals > arthropods > insects'. An *array*, as we have seen already, is a series of sister classes all at the same rank, like 'arachnids, crustaceans, insects'.

3.4.2 Parts

Types are the most classical structure in hierarchical trees, but not the only possible one. Consider this tree:

arthropods
    crustaceans
    insects
        antennae
        legs
        wings.

Now, *wings* is indeed subordinated to *insects* – it is a narrower term of *insects* – but not a kind of insects. While you can say that 'some arthropods are insects', you cannot say that 'some insects are wings'. Wings are not a type of insects, but a *part* (or component, or organ) of them. If we were to continue subdividing insects into types, the resulting subclasses should be like *hymenoptera*, a type of insects including ants and bees.

Still, many hierarchies incorporate both types and parts into the same tree, for practical purposes. A common case is that of geographical entities, which are actually parts of their broader terms rather than types of them:

> *United Kingdom*
>   *England*
>   *Wales*
>   *Scotland*
>   *Northern Ireland.*

Clearly you cannot say that *Wales* is a type of *United Kingdom*, as it in fact is a part of it. It can be further subdivided into administrative units, which again are its parts. This tree is obviously a useful one, even though it does not consist of types. (Types are related to parts in subtle ways. If we change this tree into one of people, we could probably claim that *Welsh people* are a type of *British people*, as some British people also are Welsh people, and all Welsh people are British people.)

Parts are a very important structure in the organization of geographical entities, as well as in that of organisms (which take their very name from the fact of consisting of several organs) or of artifacts (vehicles have such parts as chassis, bodywork and engine, which in turn have various parts). Parts occur in virtually every kind of entity. Some KOSs incorporate parts in hierarchical trees of NTs, while others differentiate them as a special structural element, as is usually done in facet analysis (see section 3.5).

3.4.3 Instances

Finally, hierarchical trees can include relationships between a class and an individual member of that class. Individuals are labeled by proper names, like *Jack Mills* or *United Kingdom*. For example, in the following tree:

> *polities*
>   *national states*
>   *France*
>   *United Kingdom*
>   *England*
>   *Wales*

national states is a type of *polities*, but *United Kingdom* is an instance of *national states*, that is, an individual national state. As *United Kingdom* is further divided into its parts, the tree includes cases of all three kinds of hierarchical relationship – types, parts, instances.

Instances often occur at the bottom of hierarchical trees, as *Socrates* and *Plato* are at the bottom of Porphyry's Tree. Indeed, individuals cannot be further subdivided into types – there are no types of Socrates or types of United Kingdom. They can be subdivided only into parts, like *England* and *Wales* in our example. A hierarchical tree of philosophers could include such a chain as 'philosophers > ancient philosophers > ancient Greek philosophers > Plato', consisting of a series of types which ends with an instance.

3.5 Facets

Hierarchical trees cover a variety of relationships between concepts, including types, parts and instances. They thus provide an excellent backbone for a KOS and are widespread in all domains as a way of mastering the core of their knowledge. At the same time, they have often been criticized because they force all concepts into a rigid grid that admits only of vertical relationships. A given concept must be a subclass of one or another class, and no other relationship is possible. Schemes based on this, like the classical bibliographic classifications, are described as *enumerative*, as they simply enumerate concepts in lists of classes and their subclasses.

A more refined option is to analyze a set of concepts into a wider range of internal relationships. Let us say that we are organizing knowledge about animals. Besides such subdivisions as *molluscs* or *arthropods* we may find such concepts as 'digestion'. Digestion is not a type of animals, nor a part or an instance of them. We can qualify it as a physiological process.

It can be useful to list all physiological processes that occur in animals, like *digestion, respiration, circulation* and *excretion*. A thesaurus would label them as *related terms* (*RT*) of *animals*:

> *animals*
> > RT *animal physiological processes*
> > > NT *digestion*
> > > NT *respiration.*

Related terms can be listed for each term or class and used as 'see also' suggestions so as to navigate the schedules looking for the most appropriate concepts. In *facet analysis*, a method introduced in the 1930s by Ranganathan – although anticipated to some extent by Paul Otlet and Julius Otto Kaiser – physiological processes are a *facet* of animals.

A facet can have one out of several *foci*:

mq	animals
mq95	animals, *physiological process*
mq95d	animals, digestion
mq95e	animals, respiration.

Every class can have its own typical set of facets. Besides physiological processes, other facets of animals may be growth stage and habitat. In ILC notation, facets are expressed by numerals and their foci by further letters:

mq	animals
mq926	animals, living in *habitat*
mq926r	animals, living in forests [etc.]
mq95	animals, *physiological process*
mq95d	animals, digestion [etc.]
mq97	animals, with *organ*
mq97do	animals, with stomach [etc.]
mq98	animals, *stage*
mq98g	animals, larvae
mq98n	animals, young
mq98p	animals, adult.

Notice that the facet of organs covers animal parts, which are handled here as a facet rather than a subclass as in enumerative trees above. This enables separating types and parts more clearly. As parts and other facets are introduced by numerals, they will be listed before types, following a principle already formulated by Ramus (in Ong, 1983, 249): 'the most general definition will be first, distribution next, and, if this latter is manifold, division into integral parts comes first, then division into species'.

The nice feature of facets is that they can be combined, thus producing a compound concept. This method is described as *analytico-synthetic*: knowledge is first analyzed into its facets, then the appropriate facets are synthesized to produce the suitable meaning:

mq98n95d926r animals, young, digestion, living in forests.

This procedure enables the expression of quite complex and detailed combinations of concepts, such as 'digestion in young animals living in forests', which would hardly be listed in an enumerative system, as providing for all possible combinations of concepts would imply the production of very long and unpractical schedules. Supporters of facet analysis proudly notice that, on the contrary, the schedules of their systems are much shorter than those of enumerative ones.

Facets of one class can also be applied to all its subclasses:

mq926r	animals, living in forests
mqr926r	arthropods, living in forests
mqrd926r	arachnids, living in forests
mqri926r	insects, living in forests.

3.5.1 Fundamental categories

Experience with facet analysis has shown that when collecting terminology and concepts from the literature of a given domain, like animals in our example, these tend to group into facets quite easily and naturally. Concepts in zoology can thus be grouped into the facets of physiological processes, of habitats, of developmental stages, etc. The method has been illustrated well by Vickery (1960), one of the members of the CRG, who have introduced the idea of facet analysis, originally conceived for Indian libraries by Ranganathan, into Europe.

If we analyze a different domain, say politics, we will identify other facets that are typical of it, such as official procedures, institutions and their departments, kinds of regime, etc.:

t	polities
t95	polities, *procedure*
t95t	polities, voting [etc.]
t97	polities, with *departments*
t97h	polities, with legislature
t97j	polities, with government [etc.]
t99	polities, under *regulation*
t99p	polities, under penal law
t99s	polities, under constitutional law [etc.].

From these we can construct such compounds as *t99s97h95t* 'polities, constitutional law, legislature, voting'.

Facets of animals and facets of polities are obviously different. However, if we compare them we notice that both include a processual facet (physiological process and procedures) and a composition facet (organs and departments). These belong, in a broader sense, to the same *fundamental categories*.

Ranganathan (1967) has identified five fundamental categories, which he has called 'personality', 'matter', 'energy', 'space' and 'time', famously abbreviated in the acronym 'PMEST'.

In our examples both physiological processes and political procedures belong to the category of energy, as they express some dynamic phenomena. In Ranganathan's Colon Classification all energy facets are introduced by a colon (whence the name of this KOS); in ILC the analogous category of 'transformation' is introduced by 95 (or just 5 for common facets, see section 3.5.4). The colon or the digits 95 are called the *facet indicators* for energy/transformation facets.

The names of fundamental categories are meant to have a very broad sense, as they must apply to very different domains. Thus, 'matter' covers not only the materials of which something consists but also other properties or parts of it; and 'personality' means not just a person but any entity that is the main object of enquiry in a domain, so that the personality of zoology is animal groups and the personality of political science is polities. Broad interpretation explains how such a limited list of categories can express all kinds of facets.

However, CRG members found that the PMEST set of categories was too short. Based on their experience with applying facet analysis to the development of faceted classifications for a number of special domains, Vickery (1960) and other CRG members proposed revised lists of categories, including thing (equivalent to Ranganathan's personality), kind, part, property, material, process (a spontaneous transformation in the thing), operation (an energy actively directed on the thing), agent, place and time.

While other systems have their own lists of categories, they can usually be referred more or less to this one. This seems to suggest that such categories reflect some basic cognitive structures, in the same way as the logical analysis of linguistic sentences does: indeed, any sentence is about some subject (the thing) having some attributes (kind, part, property), made of some substance (material), doing something (process) or undergoing some action (operation) by some external factor (agent), in some spatial (place) and temporal (time) context. Of course, not all categories are mandatorily expressed in all sentences: 'Yvette runs in the street' expresses only a personality, an energy and a space.

3.5.2 Citation order of facets

Facets are very useful for grouping the relevant concepts of a given domain under a small number of categories and expressing them consistently. Within every facet, as we have said, concepts will be listed in a standard order that follows some of the principles of helpful sequence:

mq95d	digestion
mq95e	respiration
mq95i	circulation.

To express a compound subject, such as 'digestion in the stomach of forest insects', it can be analyzed into the corresponding facets and foci and expressed by their facet indicators (95, etc.) and specific digit (d, etc.).

However, to ensure consistency in an index or a collection of documents the different facets should also be cited in a standard order. Clearly, the facets that are cited first will affect the position of the document in the general order more than those cited last. This gives rise to the problem of which categories deserve to be considered more relevant for determining the proximity of a document to other documents: should we first group animals by their organs, then divide them by physiological processes and habitat; or should we first group them by habitat; or what else?

Ranganathan and his followers have provided an answer in the very sequence of the *PMEST* acronym or its equivalents: personality/thing should be the first-cited facet, followed by kind, part, property, etc. This is because the attributes expressed by facets of kind and part have been found to be more strictly associated with the things to hand, as compared to their processes, and these in turn are more essential than such external factors and contexts as agents, places and times. The stomach of an insect is always associated with the insect, even if the insect is removed from the forest and taken to a laboratory. The same is true if no digestion process is happening: the insect still has a stomach.

Thus, the best option is to cite the facets in this order:

mqri97do95d926r 'insects, stomach, digestion, living in forests'.

Here is the standard citation order of facet categories in ILC:

99   of *kind*
98   as *form*
97   with *part*
96   having *property*
95   undergoing *transformation*
94   despite *disorder*
93   affected by *agent*
92   in *place*
91   at *time*.

Notice that the notation has been devised in such a way that the facets to be cited first, like 97 for parts, have a greater ordinal value than those to be cited last, like 92 for place. This is so as to follow an important principle of facet analysis, called the *principle of inversion*: so to say, 'the last shall be first'. In other words, the 'horizontal' citation order of facets within a compound subject will be the opposite of their 'vertical' order in a list of subjects. You can grasp this by examining the places of facet *-926r* 'in forests' in the following list of faceted subjects that have been sorted mechanically according to their classmarks:

mqri	insects
mqri926r	insects, in forests
mqri95d	insects, digestion
mqri95d926r	insects, digestion, in forests
mqri97do	insects, stomach
mqri97do926r	insects, stomach, in forests
mqri97do95d	insects, stomach, digestion
mqri97do95d926r	insects, stomach, digestion, in forests.

As a list or a library shelf has only one linear dimension, some related subjects that share one facet are inevitably separated, as in the case of 'insects, in forests' and 'insects, stomach, in forests'. (To retrieve all of them in an information system, a truncated query like *mqri*926r* will be needed.) However, the standard citation order of categories ensures that the foci of the most relevant facets, such as that of organs, are grouped in an optimal way. Following the standard citation order maximizes the likelihood of producing the most helpful sequences in a linear world.

3.5.3 Sources of foci

Every facet can have a variety of foci, of which our examples have listed only a small sample. The facet of physiological processes can take digestion as its value, but also respiration, or circulation, or hormone transmission, or neural transmission, or excretion, etc. These foci are defined in the specific context of animals: indeed, there is no digestion in transportation, nor in traditional dance. They are *context-defined foci*.

On the other hand, some facets provide for foci that are not defined in the same of their class. Take forests as the place where insects live. Forests are not exclusive of animals, as there are also transportation in forests and traditional dances in forests. We call these *extra-defined foci*.

In the economy of a KOS it is useful for extra-defined foci to be taken from the corresponding schedule, rather than being defined and listed again, perhaps with a different terminology and notation. For example, in Colon Classification the class of literature is first divided by a language facet: English literature, French literature and so on. The foci for this facet are then taken from the schedule of languages, which are listed in another section of the scheme.

Non-faceted schemes (also called enumerative schemes), such as Dewey, are less consistent in the use and recombination of their notation. However, they often have a similar mechanism in the form of *parallel divisions*: indeed, literature in Dewey is divided into:

820   English literature
830   German literature
840   French literature [etc.],

which parallels the order and second digit of the divisions of linguistics:

420   English language
430   Germanic languages
440   French language [etc.].

Extra-defined foci can in turn be distinguished between *special* and *general*. In the example above the value of the habitat facet is necessarily an environment – it cannot be a bicycle or a novel. The notation for it will always be taken from that for habitats. This allows cutting out the obvious implicit part meaning 'regions of the contemporary Earth' and keeping only the letters expressing their subdivisions:

ny	ecosystems
nyc	oceanic zones
nym	wetlands
nyr	forests
nyt	grasslands;

mq926 [ny]	animals, living in *habitat*
mq926c	animals, living in oceanic zones
mq926m	animals, living in wetlands
mq926r	animals, living in forests
mq926t	animals, living in grasslands.

This is an example of special extra-defined foci. On the other hand, some facets can have foci taken from any other part of the schedules, that is, general extra-defined foci:

qs	sentences
qs8	sentences, about *object*
qs8mq	sentences, about animals
qs8vx	sentences, about transport
qw8xn	sentences, about dance.

3.5.4 Common facets

Up to now our examples of facets have been specific of a particular domain or class – facets of animals, facets of polities, etc. This is also true for the habitat facet of animals, which specifies where the wild specimens of a certain group of animals are distributed and can be found. A different class, such as that of stars, will have no habitat facet – there are no stars living in wetlands or in forests. Of course, stars can have a place facet, but its foci will have to be taken from some other schedule, like the schedule of galaxies.

There are certain facets that can be associated to almost all classes. If we take places in a more general sense, to mean, for example, animals occasionally located in forests rather than always living in forests, this can be expressed by a common facet simply connecting the class of animals with that of forests, without any specific semantic implication:

mq2nyr	animals, in forests
vx2nyr	transport, in forests
xn2nyr	dance, in forests.

Unlike special facets, common facets can be attached to any class to specify its meaning. They are used very commonly, especially in the cases of place, time and form facets, which had already been identified in the early times of modern enumerative classifications. Indeed, they can also be found in such non-faceted systems as LCC or DDC. In Dewey, common facets are known as 'common subdivisions' and are often introduced by -0; for example, *590.94* means 'zoology, in Europe'; other common facets enable specifying that the subject is treated in a dictionary (*590.3*), or in a serial (*590.5*), or in a theoretical way (*590.1*).

Common facets are also used to specify verbal subject headings, as in *animals – Europe – 19th century – atlases*. In this example the basic subject is followed by a common facet of place, one of time and one of form. Forms are specifications of the document type or format in which the subject is treated; that is, they belong to the dimension δ of documents (see section 2.4). In ILC, dimensions other than phenomena can be connected to phenomena by facet indicators starting with *0*. The dimension of documents is introduced by *00*:

mq00ytg	animals, as attested in maps
mq00ytm	animals, as attested in videos,

and a further *0* connects phenomena to the next dimension, that of collections:

mq000yvl	animals, as collected in libraries
mq000yvm	animals, as collected in expositions.

3.6 Themes

Up to now we have assumed that a knowledge resource deals with just one specific subject. However, in many cases this is not true. Indeed, several *themes* can be present in one and the same source. This is increasingly likely as we move from simple sources, such as a short message, to larger and more complex ones. An academic paper usually focuses on one specific, faceted theme, like 'digestion in the stomach of insects', with possible connections to other themes. In a monograph there is enough room to treat several themes and to compare and connect them, although usually referring to a main argument which is given in the introduction and conclusions.

3.6.1 Base theme and particular themes

The identification and analysis of themes in a document is studied in text linguistics, a branch with some connections to KO. Although this field of investigation is as yet poorly developed, authors such as Alberto Cheti have introduced text linguistics into the theory of subject indexing (Cheti, 1994; 1996).

In this approach a text (which we may take here in a broad sense, to include also moving images, audio sources, etc.) has a *base theme* that is the focus of its argument, and possibly a number of other *particular themes*. For example, it could focus on the biology of certain crustaceans as its base theme but also deal with pollution of the sea where they live, which may lead the authors to devote a chapter to pollution factors, including waste management on the nearby coast, the impact of shipping routes and so on. These particular themes in themselves do not belong to biology, but to administration, transportation or even politics.

If we are to index such a knowledge resource it may be useful to account for all of its relevant themes, because in the future someone who is researching, for example, waste management could usefully retrieve this resource even though they are not a biologist. This is a typical example of the needs of inter-disciplinarity (Szostak et al., 2016).

However, the base theme should still be given priority, as it makes more sense for the resource to be grouped (e.g. on the library shelves or in a printed bibliography) with others about crustaceans than with resources about waste management. The base theme can then be expressed before the particular themes:

mqrh ve wvlh   crustaceans; conservation; ships.

Traditional library classifications have been developed with the original purpose of arranging books on shelves, so that one theme has to be chosen in order to select the appropriate shelf. For this reason some classifications do not provide for the expression of particular themes. However, it is common in cataloging practice to come across books that really do deal with two or three themes, and it is not always easy to decide which one should be chosen. In my science and technology library, for example, this is often the case with books discussing the mathematical and physical laws of statics, on which the construction of certain types of buildings is based: in some of them the physical treatment prevails, in others it is the engineering treatment, or even its application to architecture (discussing the functional requirements of buildings to serve certain practical and aesthetic purposes).

One usual solution, although not recommended officially, is to assign several classmarks to the same resource: both a physics and an engineering classmark, or both a biology and a management one. From the viewpoint of KO structural principles, we should acknowledge that they are but different themes of the same resource.

3.6.2 Phase relationships and free facets

Some more advanced KOSs do provide for such common situations. For the sixth edition of his Colon Classification, Ranganathan defined five *phase relationships*, that is, connections between different themes. These are: general relationship, bias, comparison, difference and influence. They are useful for expressing the subject of monographs, such as 'physics for engineers', 'engineering applied to architecture', 'philosophy compared with religion' and so on. UDC also provides a symbol (the colon) to express a relationship between any two classes, i.e., a general phase relationship.

A similar result can be obtained in practice by assigning several classmarks of another system, like Dewey, to the same resource, although in this case there is no hint as to which is the base theme and which are particular themes – is that physics for engineers, or engineering using some principles of physics? Is it philosophy as compared to religion, or the other way around?

As one considers different types of phase relationships the question of fundamental categories may arise again. In the same way as we have seen for special facets, one may realize that a relationship of influence belongs to the fundamental category of agents. This may lead us to refine the simple series of themes freely cited one after the other to a *freely-faceted* structure of themes connected by more-specific phase relationships:

mqrh0wvlh	crustaceans, as related (in general) to ships
mqrh2wvlh	crustaceans, on ships
mqrh3wvlh	crustaceans, affected by ships
mqrh4wvlh	crustaceans, disturbed by ships.

Now, suppose that a certain species of crustacean sticks on ships' hulls and in time causes some kind of chemical corrosion to them. The appropriate order of themes will then be different:

> *wvlh4mqrh*   ships, disturbed by crustaceans.

These examples show how the citation order of themes, or their connection through free facets, is able to express a variety of relationships between concepts.

3.6.3 Rhemes

When a relationship is expressed it is still neutral information in terms of what is asserted about reality. The last example merely informs us that some damage to ships by crustaceans is discussed. However, a study that is indexed under these themes could conclude, after various empirical and statistical evaluations, that the crustaceans cause no significant damage to ships. This fact cannot be expressed by the classmark above.

   If one wants to express the actual occurrence (or non-occurrence) of a certain relationship, themes have to be completed with *rhemes*. In text linguistics rhemes (also called *comments*) are the new information that is asserted about a theme. Both individual sentences in natural languages and whole intellectual works are usually structured by the presentation of a theme ('we will talk about ships') followed by the enunciation of a rheme ('they are indeed disturbed by crustaceans'). In a sentence the theme corresponds to the subject ('ships', 'as for ships') and the rheme corresponds to the predicate ('are disturbed by crustaceans').

   Only a limited number of KOSs allow the expression of this kind of statement in addition to the simple indication of a subject:

> *wvlh4mqrh*   ships, disturbed by crustaceans
> *wvlh4Ymqrh*   ships are disturbed by crustaceans.

3.6.4 How much syntax is needed?

Freely faceted structures were studied a great deal in the second half of the 20th century, producing some highly sophisticated KOSs such as Derek Austin's PRECIS and Jean-Claude Gardin's Syntol. With the advent of computers and digital information, however, many have found that individual themes, like 'crustaceans' or 'ships', can easily be extracted from databases using simple Boolean queries – that is, queries that can have only a positive result (both searched words occur in an index) or a negative one (they do not occur together).

   Specifying the kind of relationships between themes requires an additional procedure that has often been considered too costly, as it involves a greater amount of intellectual effort by indexers. However, relationships can still be relevant, especially when indexing specialized resources for which the order and nature of the relationship do make a difference.

It has also been observed that relationships are of special relevance in such 'soft' domains as social and human sciences: indeed, such themes as 'education', 'religion' and 'sociology' can be connected in many different ways which are not equivalent at all from the viewpoint of knowledge users. Meaningful examples have been discussed concerning such subjects as 'parents of blind children' or 'children of blind parents': in these cases, simple Boolean word searches are not enough to extract the resources that are relevant to a particular information need. On the other hand, in such 'hard' sciences as physics or engineering the connection between elements is often implicit in the subject itself: 'airplanes', 'engines' and 'turbine' can be connected in only one meaningful way, so that specification of the relationships among them may be redundant.

These examples make clear how the expression of knowledge structures can be more or less useful, depending on its context. One can develop and use very simple KOSs and apply them successfully for one's purposes, or may need more sophisticated systems that are capable of expressing hierarchies, facets, themes and rhemes, while also being more demanding in terms of the time and training needed to learn and apply them. The next chapter reviews the different KOS types and their main features.

CHAPTER 4

Knowledge organization systems (KOSs)

4.1 The notion of KOS

In order to perform KO we need some schemes according to which subjects can be ordered. Any such scheme, whether simple or complex, is called a *knowledge organization system*.

This term is relatively recent, being connected with the increasing acknowledgment of KO as a unified field (see section 1.4.7). It has been spreading especially in the context of information representation and management on the world wide web, where a variety of conceptual tools are now described by this name. People thus discuss networked KOSs in a long-living series of workshops, and publish schemes in the SKOS format (see section 5.4).

In a similar way, the term *controlled vocabulary* (see section 3.2) is also used. Both a simple list of country names and a rich thesaurus can work as controlled vocabularies, stored in tables that can be related to other tables in the global data network; for example, the name of a product can be associated with the country where it is produced, and the label for the country will be taken from a controlled vocabulary of countries to ensure data consistency. However, the notion of KOS is broader than that of controlled vocabulary, as there are KOSs consisting of non-controlled labels, such as simple keywords.

Actually, schemes for organizing knowledge have existed since long before the term *KOS* appeared. Some decades ago they were often called *indexing languages*, as they usually consisted of words (or symbols working in a way similar to words) and worked according to morphological and syntactical rules that can also be found in the grammar of natural languages. Hutchins (1975) has a good discussion of the linguistic properties of KOSs.

Other terms that are often used to generically denote KOSs are *classification* (especially in a traditional or scientific context), *taxonomy* (especially in the context of website information architecture) and *ontology* (especially in computer science). Unfortunately, the term chosen depends more often on the cultural background of the author than on any differences in intended meanings. While all these terms may occasionally be meant as synonyms of *KOS*, they should properly denote different, specific KOS types. Therefore we will use them in their specific senses, which are discussed in detail in the following sections of this chapter.

4.2 The collection dimension of a KOS

As we saw in section 1.4, a substantive part of KO theory has developed from the practical needs of organizing information about books or other printed documents, as in library catalogs or bibliographies. Thus, bibliographic classification schemes are sometimes considered as the most classic kind of KOS. In such KOSs, categories are assumed to be the classes of subjects discussed in a printed document: there can be books on philosophy, books on music, books on Chinese plates and so on. Auxiliaries and facets include such specifications as 'reference work' or 'classic', which make sense in the context of a library.

However, members of the CRG have observed that classifying books on Chinese plates is not the same as classifying Chinese plates themselves (CRG, 1978). For Chinese plates, such concepts as 'reference work' or 'classic' do not make sense. The structure of the resulting KOSs may then be different in each case.

While bibliographic classifications are a classic example, KOSs are also developed for very different kinds of collections. Chinese plates may be collected in an art history museum or gallery, where they will be organized by such KOSs as the Art and Architecture Thesaurus (AAT) or the Nomenclature for Museum Cataloging (Dunn and Bourcier, 2019), which list objects rather than books about them.

Ideally, the concept of Chinese plates in these systems (that is, their phenomena dimension, β) should be linked somehow to the same concept in a bibliographic classification (Gnoli, 2010), although in practice the words *Chinese plates* in natural language are the only common way to search in both sources. Still, KOSs for objects and KOSs for books about them can have reciprocal influences, as in the case of musical instruments as listed in a bibliographic classification or in the Hornbostel-Sachs Classification of instruments (Lee, Robinson and Bawden, 2019). Another way of promoting interoperability across knowledge dimensions is to map a class or term, such as *Chinese plates* or *flutes*, to a corresponding one in a different KOS – a practice that is increasingly encouraged in the context of linked open data.

Other KOSs that list actual objects are scientific taxonomies of living organisms. Their classes are directly classes of phenomena, such as a given family of plants, rather than perspectives, documents or their collections. Scientific taxonomies – of organisms, of celestial objects, of soils, of languages or any other phenomena – have indeed been another important factor in the historical development of KO, as we saw in section 1.4.

The variety of collection types for which KOSs are available can be appreciated by browsing the Basel Register of Taxonomies, Ontologies and Classifications

(BARTOC), an extensive online directory of thousands of KOSs which includes systems conceived for libraries, for museums, for schools, for institutional documentation and so on. KOSs in BARTOC are themselves indexed by common schemes (DDC, ILC and EuroVoc are used): these need to be differentiated not just by their phenomena covered and perspectives, but also by their intended application (dimensions of document type, collection, information need and people). For example, two KOSs may both cover health care, but while one is intended for purposes of bibliographic search and retrieval, the other may be intended for evaluating the quantity and quality of medical research in a specific country, which will make their structure and granularity different.

4.3 Special and general KOSs

Another important difference is that between special and general KOSs.

Special KOSs focus on a specific domain of knowledge, of whatever broadness: a specific academic discipline, or a very restricted technical field, or a leisure sector. There are KOSs devoted to agriculture, to the arts, to procedures and components in the manufacture of spectacles, or to fantasy videogames.

In a special KOS the concepts and terminology that form the core of the domain are given priority and covered in great detail. This allows it to provide terminology and relationships for specific concepts, such as the technical names of certain components or the jargon for certain game subcultures, that are rarely provided in a general KOS, where one would simply find broad terms such as *manufacturing* or *videogames*. Domain specialists usually find that special KOSs are more effective in providing all the detail they need to index their own field, while general KOSs do not.

While the selected field is at the center of a special scheme, concepts and terms from other fields are always needed – although probably in lesser detail – inasmuch as they interact with the core concepts. A KOS on the manufacture of spectacles, besides focusing on types of spectacles and factory procedures, will also need some basic concepts concerning optics, types of sight disorders, plastic materials, economics and enterprise management. As spectacles are to be used by people, at least a simple vocabulary of people categories, such as *children* or *women*, will also be needed. Aesthetic facets will involve concepts, such as colors and raw materials, that are not exclusive to the manufacture of spectacles. Thus, while adopting a perspective focused on a particular domain, a special KOS will be connected to several other domains. In this sense, Foskett (1991) has argued that even special classifications somehow imply general classifications.

This idea leads us to look at general systems. While they provide less detail, they do offer other advantages related to their capability of providing an overview of all knowledge and of connections among its parts. With a general KOS you may not be able to express a concept with full precision, but you should always be able to situate it in a general map and visualize its relationships with other areas.

General concepts also have an important role in teaching, as they can offer a view of where a specific subdiscipline treated in a textbook or a course is placed within the whole of knowledge. Awareness of interdisciplinary connections is increasingly acknowledged as a basic requirement for schools of all grades.

Organizing the whole of knowledge in consistent ways is obviously not an easy task. Various strategies have been developed over the course of history, as we saw in section 1.4: from traditional lists of academic disciplines, to philosophical principles that can guide the ordering of subjects. During the 20th century it became common to call such KOSs 'universal' classification schemes, as in the names of the Universal Decimal Classification, Ejnar Wåhlin's Universal System and Martin Scheele's Universal Faceted Classification, and in Ingetraut Dahlberg's research on 'the universal classification system of knowledge' (Dahlberg, 1974).

As was discussed in section 2.4.4, recent decades have seen an increased awareness of the relativity of cultural assumptions, making most KO researchers skeptical about the possibility of truly universal – that is, acceptable to everybody – systems. We then prefer to adopt the more neutral term *general* as opposed to *special*, being aware of the risks implied in claiming that any particular system is 'universal'.

4.4 KOS types

Now that we have made clear what we mean by *KOS*, and what the various possible approaches and applications of KOSs are, we need to review the different existing KOS types.

As we have mentioned, some of them are classics in KO history, such as philosophical classifications of the sciences, bibliographical classifications and subject heading lists. However, especially since the middle of the 20th century, many other KOS types have been introduced, possibly reflecting the growing need for organizing the increasing amount of information and data treated in many institutions. Documentation services have developed *thesauri*, a kind of middle way between classifications and alphabetical subject headings lists. Information architects have adopted the term *taxonomy* and introduced it in the new context of knowledge management. Computer scientists have developed sophisticated structures that they call *ontologies*, a term so in fashion today that it is often misapplied to a wide variety of other KOSs. Researchers in such other fields as psychology, linguistics and information science have created other terms (*topic maps*, *conceptual maps*, *knowledge graphs* and so on) for what basically are varieties of KOSs and applications of them.

This situation is quite confusing, as we have noted already, especially considering that all these tools share a core of basic principles, which we reviewed in the previous chapter. Knowing this, and now being aware of the general idea of KOSs, we will explore what makes the main KOS types different. As we shall see, the issue is not one of choosing among alternative, opposing principles, as the core principles are common. Rather, it is which particular structures (lists, hierarchies, facets, etc.) are implemented and given priority, and which are not.

One might wonder why a KOS should not adopt *all* available structures and known principles, in order to achieve an optimal efficiency. In response to that, remember that every additional structure, however powerful, also adds complexity to the system, making it more demanding to learn, implement and use. A system with a longer learning curve, like a wide ontology, will be costly for both indexers and end users. Is there a real need to invest so much time, energy and perhaps money just to be able to use it?

The good answer is 'it depends'! It depends indeed on what one can and wants to do with the information one is treating. While sophisticated services do need a careful representation of reality, such as that in a faceted classification or an ontology, simpler and quicker systems may suffice for less ambitious services, like indexing user-generated content on the web in social networks or video platforms. It would be utopian to hope that posts in a forum or shared images on Instagram could ever be indexed accurately and consistently by someone, be it a large team of specialized indexers or the mass of users, who will never share any common methodology and motivation level, as each is using the service for different reasons and in a different way. This is why the existence of different KOS types is a good thing, and the best general strategy is simply to know about all of them.

4.4.1 Keyword systems and folksonomies

The simplest way to describe the content of a document is to associate it with one or more words. Indeed, words are the meaningful units of language (see section 3.1).

A word chosen to describe or retrieve the subject content of a document is known as a *keyword*. It can be *derived* from the document itself, or *assigned* to it after its content has been examined. Derived keywords can be extracted from the title, the abstract or the full text, as they are identified as being especially representative of the contents.

For example, an automatic statistical analysis can identify a set of words that occur frequently in the text but are quite rare overall in a reference corpus of texts. Suppose that the analysis of a text, either intellectual or automatic (see section 6.3), has led to the identification of some representative keywords, such as *spider*, *Namibia* and *biodiversity*. These keywords can then be associated with a document and simply listed, e.g. in alphabetical order:

biodiversity; Namibia; spider.

This kind of basic indexing is often required of the authors themselves when they submit an article for a conference or an academic journal. Indeed, in very specialized domains authors are among the most knowledgeable persons concerning the topic of an article, while external indexers would have only a more general knowledge of it and could be less precise.

A similar situation occurs with content published on large platforms on the internet, like posts on personal blogs, Facebook or Twitter, images on Instagram or videos on YouTube. Given their huge quantity, it would be impossible for them to be indexed by external specialists. The only hope of organizing them in some way is by inviting authors and other users to provide them with *tags*, that is, representative words describing their content.

Because in various platforms such words are distinguished from other words in the text by starting with a hash character, they have become known as *hashtags*. Hashtags are nothing but keywords. A video documentary on the life of some African spider uploaded to the web may be tagged *#biodiversity #Namibia #spider*, just as an academic paper on a similar topic.

Hashtags have become part of internet culture, to the point that they are also used as a means to express other than just subject content: such hashtags as *#showmustgoon* or *#goodtoknow* are pseudo-headings that refer to contemporary shared contexts, commenting on them, often in an ironical sense.

An interesting feature of internet content is that it can be edited or commented on publicly by other users. This increases the hope that good indexing will be produced, as an individual author may not be sufficiently skilled or motivated to produce valuable tags. As more users provide tags for the same document a corpus of useful keywords can be developed. This is the idea behind systems of tags that have been called *folksonomies* – by altering the word *taxonomy* (actually meaning quite a different KOS type: see section 4.4.2) to mean that this kind of KOS is produced by the people. The term implies that such a system is a very democratic one, as anybody can add their own tags without being forced by the normative power of some central institution, as is common in traditional KO (Quintarelli, 2005).

Clearly, as anyone can add their own tags without limitations, consistency of the system is left to the good willingness of taggers. For example, someone might add a *#towatch* tag to the video in the example above in order to remember that they want to watch it later, a tag useful only to themselves and not related to the content; another user might tag it as *#ugly*, a description with which spider specialists will not agree.

Consistency is also a matter of word morphology and lexicon (see section 3.2): while some users may adopt the tag *#spider*, others may use *#spiders*, so that some of the relevant documents will be missing from the results of either search. This problem can be observed even among KO specialists when they use hashtags!

While the first attendees at the 16th International ISKO Conference in Aalborg in 2022 may identify their tweets from the conference as *#ISKO16*, others may independently start to tag their tweets *#ISKO2022*. Wise conference organizers sometimes recommend a specific hashtag from the very beginning so as to enforce consistency – that is, they apply the old principle of vocabulary control.

Another limitation of keywords as assigned by authors themselves, or by other users, is that they violate what Riccardo Ridi (2013) has called the *indexer thirdness*. Traditional practices, where external indexers choose index terms on the basis of some standard principle, mean that the indexers act as a neutral third party between content creators and users. When indexing is up to content creators themselves, they may exploit this to their own advantage, for example by claiming that their video material is *#exclusive* and *#previously_unpublished*, when it is not; or even by providing fake, misleading information.

To counter such problems, while keeping the openness and power of folksonomies, some projects have attempted to couple open editing by users with various forms of check, such as automatically recommending tags that have already been used in the system on the basis of some textual description, or matching user-generated tags with some more controlled KOS, like a taxonomy or a thesaurus (Matthews et al., 2010; Golub et al., 2014; Johansson and Golub, 2019).

We will now discuss these more advanced KOS types.

4.4.2 Taxonomies

In taxonomies, words identifying classes of entity are slightly more organized than in keyword systems, as they are arranged in a hierarchy. *Spiders* is not an isolated keyword anymore, but is part of a hierarchy of living forms:

> *animals*
> > *arachnids*
> > > *acari*
> > > *scorpions*
> > > *spiders*
> > *arthropods*
> > *molluscs*
> > ...

This provides users with an intuitive structure that can be browsed quickly to find the relevant items. The hierarchy is usually based on the genus–species relationship. However, there is no absolute rule, as whole–part or other relationships can also be used if they are considered to be useful to the purposes at hand (see section 3.4).

Also, notice that, within every class, subclasses are listed in alphabetical order, so that *arthropods* precede *molluscs*, despite the fact that the latter may be considered to be more primitive in evolutionary terms. In other words, taxonomies do not manage sorting: to do this, we would need to add a notation, and hence enter into the more sophisticated KOS type of classification schemes.

Nevertheless, taxonomies are a quite simple and effective way to organize access to information. Indeed they have become widespread in the management of large websites and portals (think of Wikipedia categories), also working as site maps. They are also used to organize information in large organizations, either public or private (Hedden, 2016).

In her KOS for KO literature (www.isko.org/scheme.php), Dahlberg distinguishes class 5 'special objects classifications (taxonomies)' from 6 'special classification systems and thesauri', as the former is meant to directly organize objects, while the latter is to organize documentation about objects. Indeed, scientific taxonomies of animals, plants, minerals, soils, climates, languages, etc. have been developed within each scientific discipline, independently from library and documentation services, to organize their objects of study in a museum or to situate the position of a newly discovered species.

Having started with the pioneering work of such researchers as Gesner and Linnaeus, scientific taxonomies are now published as official KOSs, such as the International Code of Nomenclature for Algae, Fungi and Plants, the International Code of Zoological Nomenclature or the Ethnologue taxonomy of languages. Special schemes have also been developed in the humanities, such as the Aarne-Thompson-Uther system of folktale types and the Hornbostel-Sachs classification of musical instruments (which can be called a 'taxonomy' inasmuch as it lists objects, or a 'classification' as it is arranged systematically with a notation) (Lee, 2018).

4.4.3 Subject heading lists

The problem of lack of uniformity in keywords is addressed by the creation of *controlled vocabularies*, where only certain forms of words are kept, thus acquiring the status of controlled terms (see section 3.2). Alternative forms can be listed as cross-references of two types: 'A *see* B' for synonyms and other equivalent forms, or 'A *see also* B' for otherwise related terms.

This technique is often adopted in back-of-the-book indexing, where an alphabetical list of terms pointing to relevant pages in the text is provided, possibly with some cross-references.

Similar alphabetical sequences have also been developed in the catalogs of large libraries to relate a selected term to one or more books about the corresponding topic. As some libraries had very extensive collections and developed professional expertise in the production of such subject headings following consistent rules, like those published by Charles Ammi Cutter in 1876, their subject heading lists have become a kind of standard, adopted and reused for the catalogs of many other libraries.

This is especially the case with the Library of Congress (LC), an institution of the US government in Washington, DC, whose LC Subject Headings have been distributed widely, together with bibliographic descriptions indexed by them: they circulated first in the form of magnetic tapes, and then via the internet, thus becoming a practical reference tool for any English-speaking library. These developments have been enhanced by the diffusion of union OPACs, where the same headings can be linked to bibliographic descriptions of items owned by a large number of libraries.

Similar dynamics can be observed in the libraries of other countries and languages. Italian libraries mainly refer to the Soggettario of the Central National Library of Florence (BNCF), recently restructured into Nuovo Soggettario; German libraries to the Schlagwortnormdatei (SWD); French libraries to the Répertoire d'autorité-matière encyclopédique et alphabétique unifié (RAMEAU); Portuguese-speaking libraries to the Sistema de indexação em português (SIPORbase). For a long time an English alternative has been the Sears List of Subject Headings, initiated in 1923 by Minnie Earl Sears as a more accessible version of the LCSH.

When a subject heading, like *spiders*, is quite general and can be applied to tens or hundreds of documents, it is useful to specify it by some additional descriptors. For example:

spiders
spiders – habitat
spiders – habitat – Namibia
spiders – Namibia.

The simple heading should be assigned only to documents about spiders in general, such as a monographs on spiders of the world. More specific documents should be indexed with compound headings, like *spiders – habitat*. Again, this heading will be appropriate only for studies on the habitats of all spider species, while those focusing on spiders living in Namibia should be qualified with an additional geographical subdivision. This is expressed in the principle of *coextension* of indexing.

Now, let us observe the sequence in which these headings have been listed. As the principle of arrangement is alphabetical, *spiders* alone precedes all its specifications. This is appropriate in light of the KO principle that general subjects should always precede specific ones. The same principle is also applied in all subdivisions, e.g. *spiders – habitat* precedes *spiders – habitat – Namibia*.

Within the same rank of subdivision, alphabetical ordering applies again, so that *habitat* precedes *Namibia*, but *Angola* would precede *habitat*: geographical descriptors will thus be mixed with other descriptors (to group and sort them more consistently, a notation would be needed).

Within the same heading, other important rules have to be applied to the citation order of descriptors. *Spiders* precedes *habitat* because the entity which is the object of study is usually taken as the leading term. Indeed, the indexed documents are not about the ecological notion of habitat as such, but only about habitat as a facet of the biology of spiders, that is, a specification of it. The sequence would be the same in the cases of *spiders – respiration* or *spiders – conservation*. In the same way, *Namibia* works as a specification of *spiders* rather than being the main focus of these documents (while it would be the leading term for a touristic guide of Namibia).

Finally, between *habitat* and *Namibia*, the geographical specification comes later because it is considered to be less discriminating than the other facet. Geographical, chronological (*20th century* or *wet season*) and formal (*handbooks* or *checklists*) subdivisions are always cited last in compound subject headings, in this order.

As you may have noticed, such rules for citation order basically follow the same logic as in faceted classmarks (see section 3.5.2). Indeed, place, time and form are the most commonly found facets, even in systems that lack any deep facet analysis into parts, properties, processes, agents, etc. This elementary analysis into common facets has been formalized in the FAST (Faceted Application of Subject Terminology) version of the LCSH.

4.4.4 Thesauri
Another type of controlled vocabulary has become popular since the 1960s and 1970s: thesauri (Dextre Clarke, 2017). They consist of lists of controlled terms, as in subject headings, although usually only individual terms are listed, rather than combinations of terms.

As in subject heading lists, relations of equivalence between *preferred* and *non-preferred* terms are provided, using the standard codes USE (functionally equivalent to 'see') and RT (related term, equivalent to 'see also') (see section 3.2). Furthermore, hierarchical relationships (see section 3.4) are also provided, by the BT/NT (broader term/narrower term) codes:

animals
NT *arthropods*
NT *molluscs*
...;

arthropods
BT *animals*
NT *arachnids*
NT *insects*
...;

bivalves
UF *bivalvia*
UF *lamellibranchiata*
UF *pelecypoda*
BT *molluscs*;

lamellibranchiata
USE *bivalves*;

mollusca
BT *animals*
NT *bivalves*
NT *cephalopods*
NT *gastropods*
RT *shells*.

The use of such relationship symbols is prescribed in international standards. The first of these was ISO 2788, *Guidelines for the Establishment and Development of Monolingual Thesauri*, originally published in 1974 and updated in 1986, which defined relationships between terms within one and the same language. It was followed in 1985 by ISO 5964, *Guidelines for the Establishment and Development of Multilingual Thesauri*, covering relationships of equivalence between terms in different languages. Since 2011 both of these have been replaced by ISO 25964, developed after the British national standard BS 8723 and including a Part 1 on *Thesauri for Information Retrieval* and a Part 2 (issued in 2013) on *Interoperability with Other Vocabularies*.

As is well known, the meanings of many words do not map exactly across different languages. The same is sometimes true of terms used in different contexts and user communities, so it is interesting that ISO 25964 also provides for partial matching between different terms:

inexact equivalence:
horticulture ~ EQ *gardening*;

intersecting compound equivalence:
women executives EQ *women + executives;*

cumulative compound equivalence:
inland waterways EQ *rivers | canals.*

Thesauri are a tool of linguistic interest because they codify the exact terminology used in specialized domains. Indeed, thesauri often cover special domains, even in great detail. In some cases the covered domain may be broad, as with the Medical Subject Headings (MeSH) or the Art and Architecture Thesaurus (AAT), or even general, as in the Nuovo Soggettario thesaurus (originally a subject headings list, as mentioned in the previous section, but evolved into a full thesaurus including NT and RT relationships).

Given their linguistic character, thesauri lend themselves to being joined with NLP tools: words extracted from texts via statistical methods can then be matched with the terms of a thesaurus to exploit the semantic relationships recorded in them. This can help to remove ambiguity in deciding between alternative meanings of a word. *Wood* in a text can mean either a natural association of trees and other living organisms, or a material used in building and manufacturing; suppose that the thesaurus records a semantic relationship of the latter with *carpentry*: now, if *carpentry* is also found in the text to hand, the latter meaning is likely the appropriate one.

Another advanced use of thesauri is for search interfaces: when a user types a word to be searched for in a database, it can be automatically matched with those in a thesaurus, and synonyms and hyponyms can be displayed as suggestions for expanding the search. This application agrees with the findings of several studies, that users tend to choose exceedingly broad or inaccurate terms in their first search.

4.4.5 Classification schemes

Classification schemes are among the most classic KOS forms: they have been developed since antiquity, both to organize libraries and archives and to summarize the whole of knowledge or parts of it (see section 1.4).

General classifications list a set of knowledge fields – usually academic disciplines – which form the main classes. These can be sorted according to an epistemological principle (e.g., sciences of reason, of imagination, of memory) or according to an ontological principle (e.g., levels of increasing organization) (see section 2.4.5). The order is then systematic, as opposed to alphabetical as in most taxonomies and thesauri.

Main classes are divided into subclasses and so on. Both the order of sibling classes and the rank of division can be expressed by a notation (Gnoli, 2018c), although philosophical classifications of the sciences usually lack this.

mq	animals
mqn	molluscs
mqr	arthropods
mqrd	arachnids
mqrh	crustaceans
mqri	insects.

Currently, the most widespread bibliographic classifications are DDC, its derivation UDC and LCC. Other general systems are important in specific areas, such as the Library-Bibliographical Classification (LBC or BBK) in Russia (Sukyasian, 2017) and the Chinese Library Classification (Bu, 2017). All of these are usually described as basically *enumerative* systems, although some facetization has been introduced gradually in recent editions.

In fully *faceted* (see section 3.3) classifications, every main class can also be specified by a combination of attributes, its special facets: for example, in ILC *mqrd98n95d926r* 'arachnids, young, digestion, living in forests'. Faceted classifications thus allow the building of a large number of possible combinations from relatively short schedules of basic classes and facets. Their prototypes are Ranganathan's Colon Classification (Satija, 2017) and the second edition of Bliss Bibliographic Classification (BC2) edited by Jack Mills and Vanda Broughton of the CRG.

Common facets can also be appended to any main class, functioning in the same way as geographical, chronological and formal subdivisions in subject headings. Similar considerations regarding the citation order of facets apply here.

Terminology is less central in classification schemes as compared to thesauri, because the meaning of a class can be inferred by the context of its parent class (*mqrd* 'arachnids' are a type of *mqr* 'arthropods', in turn a subclass of *mq* 'animals'), sibling classes (they are arthropods other than crustaceans and insects, as these are covered by adjacent classes) and subclasses (the enumeration of the types of arachnids, including acari and spiders, provides an idea of what arachnids in general are). The verbal caption of a class thus has more of a descriptive than a defining function.

Still, modern classification schemes try to provide an accurate terminology, sometimes including synonyms and quasi-synonyms. If one adds RT-like relationships with classes in different hierarchies (e.g. between acari and parasitic diseases in medicine) the system will now incorporate all the functions of a thesaurus, thus implementing a powerful KOS variety that Bhattacharyya (1982) has called a *classaurus*.

4.4.6 Ontologies

Ontologies meant as a KOS type (as opposed to ontology as the philosophical branch dealing with what exists and its categories) are a recent development. They are aimed at representing and exploiting knowledge in formalized ways, as part of applications in computer science, including artificial intelligence (Sowa, 1999).

A large community of digital ontologists has developed, with its conferences and organizations, such as Formal Ontologies in Information Systems, the Ontology Summit, the Joint Ontology Workshops and the International Association for Ontology and its Applications.

Although not everybody is aware of it, the basic conceptual principles of ontologies, such as the identification of classes and relationships between them, are common to other KOS types (Slavic and Civallero, 2011). A greater integration of the KO community with that of ontologists is thus desirable.

The most important structural relation of ontologies is the hierarchical one ('is a'), specifying, for example, that *Spider isA Arachnid*. Formalization allows for some procedures of automatic deduction: if another relationship specifies that *Arachnid isA Arthropod*, it may be correctly inferred that *Spider isA Arthropod*. In other words, *inheritance* of properties holds for certain relationships.

However, this is not the case with all relationships, as in the case of *fatherOf*: while *CharlesMartel fatherOf PepinTheShort* is a true relationship, and *PepinTheShort fatherOf Charlemagne* is also true, *CharlesMartel fatherOf Charlemagne* is false.

As this example shows, ontologies may introduce as many relationships as are needed (similarly to faceted classifications: Broughton, 2011); additionally, ontologies specify the properties of such relationships and of the classes connected by them. Specifications may also include restrictions to the allowed arguments of a relationship: a relationship like *hasHeightInMeters* can have only a numerical value as its argument, while arguments such as *Towering* are not permitted.

Ontologies are usually developed in view of special applications in some domain, similarly to thesauri. General ontologies have also been attempted and are known as *top-level*, *upper* or *foundational ontologies*. They include Doug Lenat's Cyc, Barry Smith's Basic Formal Ontology, Heinrich Herre's General Formal Ontology (GFO) and Nicola Guarino's Descriptive Ontology for Linguistics and Cognitive Engineering (DOLCE). These are used especially to connect concepts in different special ontologies, by means of general categories that can be applied to both.

Such general categories, that is, very general classes, mostly concern functional types of concepts, such as *Things*, *Events*, *Processes* and their subdivisions (e.g. between continuous events, completed events, instantaneous events, etc.). There is less interest in organizing classes of existing things by their nature, such as material entities, living beings, mental and social entities, etc., although the notion of level of reality, which is important in several classifications, is also formalized in GFO.

Representation of classes and their relationships is implemented by formal languages. In the expanding context of the internet, these languages have taken the form of XML (Extended Markup Language)/RDF (Resource Description Framework) markup languages (see section 5.4) that can be published and exchanged across different servers. In particular, the Web Ontology Language (abbreviated as *OWL*, not *WOL*, so that it is symbolized by an owl) is used to represent ontologies in the Semantic Web.

CHAPTER 5

Representation of knowledge organization structures

5.1 Headings in paper catalogs and indexes

The subject of ontologies, which we discussed at the end of the previous chapter, has introduced the problem of the formal representation of KOSs. Although this is especially important in ontologies, some form of representation is also needed for any other KOS. This chapter will briefly discuss the main aspects of this.

When titles and headings began to be used to organize manuscript texts (which to begin with were simple strings of words and sentences), these had to be demarcated using some different graphic style. One common style was to use red ink, as opposed to black ink for main text. This practice became known as *rubrication*, from the Latin *rubrum*, 'red'.

Perhaps as a legacy from that time, subject headings were still written in red in some library card catalogs until the 20th century. For centuries, catalogs were kept in the form of books in which the subjects and titles were listed in some order (and we saw in section 1.4.1 something akin to a catalog inscribed on the walls of a library). At the end of the 18th century catalogs written on movable cards were introduced in France. A century later, the Italian businessman Aristide Staderini patented the 'Vittorio Emanuele Library' card catalog (named after the National Library in Rome that first adopted it), consisting of cards with holes punched on the left side, by means of which they could be inserted into binders. The catalog consisted of a series of such binders, each covering a section of the alphabetical or systematic order.

Later, the traditional card catalog was developed in which cards with a hole punched in the center of the bottom edge are bound together in a drawer by means of a metal crossbar. The catalog consisted of a set of such drawers arranged in one or more cabinets. Such catalogs can still be seen in many old libraries. Cards of various sizes have been used, but standard measurements became common so that new cards could be purchased or exchanged across different catalogs; the final standard international format was 12.5 × 7.5 cm.

The movable card format made it possible to insert any number of new cards into the appropriate place in the alphabetical sequence of authors or subject headings (in the less common *classified catalogs*, the order could be a systematic one, by classification notation).

Bibliographic information for each book or document was written on a card by hand or, later, was typewritten or computer-printed. The basic bibliographic elements – authors, title, place and date of publication, publisher – were arranged on the card in a standard sequence according to national – and later, international – cataloging rules, which gradually developed over time: the Anglo-American Cataloguing Rules and other national rules, the International Standard Bibliographic Description (ISBD) and, currently, the Resource Description and Access (RDA) standard. Cultural heritage and museum resources are also cataloged according to structured, usually more detailed forms.

We will not delve into these rules, which are treated in specialized handbooks and websites. What is relevant from the perspective of KO is that information elements are organized in standard sequences and in specific parts of a card or form. In particular, the top left part of a movable card records the *heading* – that is, the information according to which the cards are sorted – formulated in a standard form to avoid ambiguity: *Surname, Name* for author headings, or descriptors in a standard citation order (see sections 3.5.2 and 4.4) for subject headings. Placing the information there allows users to browse quickly through the cards, without having to read the main content of each one, until they find a relevant card. The shelfmark of the corresponding book or document is often recorded in the top right corner and directs the user or librarian to the appropriate place in the collection.

5.2 Subject authority data in online bibliographic databases

In the last decades of the 20th century catalogs gradually moved from card drawers to digital information, recorded first on magnetic tapes and then on discs. The advent of the internet enabled the sharing of bibliographic information across many libraries, so that it was sufficient for a single library to produce accurate descriptions of a resource that libraries owning other copies of the same resource could later import into their own catalogs by. In the USA a leading role was taken by the Library of Congress, which distributed its bibliographic descriptions to thousands of other libraries across the country and even abroad – a practice that heavily influenced the spread of the particular KOSs used by that library, that is, LCC, DDC and LCSH.

The elements that once were written in various places on the catalog cards – authors, title, publisher, subject, classification, shelfmark, etc. – are now distributed into the different fields of an electronic database. A main table in the database records bibliographic information for each document, divided into separate fields and subfields for title, subtitle, authors, other contributors, publication date, size, number of pages, etc. Other tables are created to record *authority lists* of authors, subjects and any other element that is useful as an access point in electronic searches – a functional equivalent of headings in catalog cards. To make searching quicker, for every authority list an inverted file can be created, rearranging the headings in alphabetical order so that they can be scanned by automatic procedures and the associated bibliographic records are retrieved instantaneously.

Databases of library catalogs, especially in universities, have been a pioneering force in the development of online information services, as they consist of millions of records that have to be stored and transmitted effectively. Catalogs that are freely available through internet terminals are known as *online public access catalogs (OPACs)*.

Interfaces for search and retrieval once consisted of simple command lines (such as *AU=shakespeare AND TI=othello*), and results were listed on a screen that could display only the characters of the ASCII set (letters, numbers, punctuation marks and a very limited set of other symbols). Later, graphical user interfaces have permitted the display of bibliographic information in user-friendly forms and navigation by a mouse-controlled pointer, as in contemporary personal computers. Web interfaces for OPACs were created and are still common.

In some large institutions bibliographic information from catalogs is merged with that from other databases, such as bibliographic references or full-text e-journals and e-books, to provide 'integrated library systems' and 'discovery tools' that allow users to perform a single search for many different functions – although losing awareness of the search mechanisms which they are using.

In order to collect bibliographic information from many different libraries in a consistent way to make it available in union catalogs, or even to exchange it across different catalogs, standard formats for recording data have become necessary. Note that these are an additional component which is different from the rules for formulating headings themselves (such as ISBD and RDA).

Let us take the case of a classmark in DDC used in a catalog as an access point to several books on spiders. The classmark for spiders in DDC is *595.44*, part of class *590* 'zoology'. The information to be recorded actually consists of at least three elements: the class number itself, its verbal caption in the language of the catalog, say English (but multilingual catalogs are often needed, especially in multilingual countries such as Canada or Switzerland); and the KOS from which the classmark has been taken, that is, DDC (*595.44* could mean something completely different in another KOS). Also, classmarks sometimes change in new KOS editions, so the appropriate DDC edition, say 22nd, should also be specified.

Standard codes for the representation and exchange of bibliographic data are known as MAchine-Readable Cataloging (MARC). MARC variants have been developed in several Western countries to record bibliographic descriptions in their respective national cataloging codes: there have been a UKMARC in the UK, a USMARC in the USA, an SBNMARC in Italy and so on. An international common format has been published with the name UNIMARC. However, in time a new US version, MARC21, has become a de facto standard even in non-US countries.

MARC formats record bibliographic information in different fields that are identified by numbers. Besides fields for authors, titles and many other details, there are some UNIMARC fields devoted to subject content, including fields 184, 250, 661–668 and 676.

Here is an example of content in the field for Classification scheme and edition:

184 0#$addc$c22.

The field number is followed by two digits that are the *indicators* of the field. The first one has value *0*, meaning that the standard edition of the KOS is used, as opposed to abridged (*1*) or other (*8*). The second indicator is not used in this field, so its position is filled with *#*. After the indicators, *subfields* begin, each identified by a dollar sign followed by a lowercase letter. Subfields for field 184 are as follows:

$a Classification scheme code
$b Edition title
$c Edition identifier
$d Source edition identifier
$e Language code
$f Authorisation
$n Variations note.

Thus, in the example above the value for subfield *$a* is *ddc*, that is, Dewey Decimal Classification, and that for subfield *$c* is *22*, that is, 22nd edition. The other subfields are not used.

UNIMARC field 250 is for class number proper. Our example is:

250 ##$a595.44$hScience$hZoology$hArthropoda$hChelicerata$j Araneida. Spiders,

including part of the subfields for 250:

$a Number or beginning of span
$c Ending number of span
$h Caption hierarchy
$j Caption
$k Summary number span caption hierarchy
$z Table identification: this subfield will appear first. Repeatable.

That is, in the example above, class number $a is 595.44 (number spans are also provided for, e.g. Arachnida span from 595.42 to 595.44); $h subfields record the whole hierarchical chain of parent classes (science, zoology, arthropoda, chelicerata), which can usefully be displayed in some applications; and subfield $j records the caption for this class.

As we saw in sections 3.5 and 4.4, notation can consist of several components – such as a basic class, common facets or special facets – that are combined to produce a detailed meaning. These elements can be exploited in a digital environment. For example, 595.4409152 'spiders in forests' is a compound of 595.44 with -09152 'in forests'. If -09152 were recorded as a separate element it could be exploited to find this document together with others on different subjects with the common specification 'in forests'.

Compound subjects are provided for by fields 661–668 for number building. UNIMARC specifications say that they 'are heavily coded and are intended for use in computer processing, to allow the system to do the necessary computations to create synthesized numbers':

661 Add or divide like instructions
Table identification
Internal subarrangement or add table entry (repeatable)
Synthesized number components
[Order in which elements are to be applied in synthesizing a class number].

Unfortunately, it is not common to find such powerful detailed information leveraged in current OPAC interfaces.

UNIMARC field 676 is another way of specifying the resource classmark for DDC as an internationally widespread KOS (fields for less common classifications such as Bliss or Colon are not provided):

676 Dewey Decimal Classification.
Occurrence: Optional. Repeatable;

Subfields:
$a Number: The number as taken from the Dewey Decimal Classification schedules.
Prime marks are indicated by /. Not repeatable.
$v Edition: The number of the edition used.
An *a* is added to the number to indicate abridged edition. Not repeatable.
$z Language of edition: The language in coded form of the edition from which the number in subfield $a is taken. For codes see Appendix A. Not repeatable.

An example for a document on spiders classified by an Italian translation of DDC 22nd edition is:

676 ##$a595.44$v22$zita.

5.3 Subject metadata of digital documents

With the proliferation of digital documents, often published on the world wide web as part of websites and digital libraries, the problem of making them findable to potential users became increasingly relevant.

Directories of web resources selected and indexed manually have been developed, starting with the still existing WWW Virtual Library and followed by Yahoo!, Dmoz (later becoming Google Directory) and many others. Such *subject gateways* have usually been organized by a taxonomy of domains listed in alphabetical order (see section 4.4.2), usually with a relatively flat structure of some 20 classes divided into subclasses, possibly to the third or fourth rank of specificity. Unlike in bibliographic classifications, domains do not necessarily correspond to academic disciplines, as they include such categories as *computers*, *food and drinks* or *games*.

This practice was a viable compromise between accurate cataloging by experts and no KO at all, as it guided users to browse subjects, and thus become aware of the functions of categorization. However, as the number of new web pages created by an increasingly wide range of people exploded, and the precision and effectiveness of Google search outperformed that of previously existing search engines, keyword search on the whole internet has, by and large, become users' preferred search approach, and subject gateways have often been abandoned.

The plan to catalog digital resources by traditional library methods is even more challenging. Experts such as Michael Gorman (2003) have argued that, as selection has always been part of the role of libraries, librarians should also select certain digital resources and describe them in catalogs along with printed resources, using such standards as ISBD(ER) (International Standard

Bibliographic Description for Electronic Resources). In practice, however, this has happened in only a small minority of initiatives.

In the case of internet documents, it soon became clear that their rate of growth and rapidity of publication and update required new, lighter forms of description, including description of their subject content. A series of meetings involving publishers, librarians and computer scientists, known as the Dublin Core Metadata Initiative (DCMI) because the first meeting was held in Dublin, Ohio in 1995, has produced a list of simple ('core') description elements that can each be associated with a digital document.

This descriptive information about documents has become known as *metadata*, that is, 'data about data', although it is just another form of traditional indexing. Some Dublin Core (DC) metadata elements also concern subject content, including the following.

- *Subject*: The topic of the resource. Typically, the subject will be represented using keywords, key phrases, or classification codes. Recommended best practice is to use a controlled vocabulary.
- *Description*: An account of the resource. Description may include but is not limited to: an abstract, a table of contents, a graphical representation, or a free-text account of the resource.

The other DC elements are as follows:

- *Title:* A name given to the resource. Typically, a Title will be a name by which the resource is formally known.
- *Creator:* An entity primarily responsible for making the resource. Examples of a Creator include a person, an organization, or a service. Typically, the name of a Creator should be used to indicate the entity.
- *Contributor*: An entity responsible for making contributions to the resource. Examples of a Contributor include a person, an organization, or a service. Typically, the name of a Contributor should be used to indicate the entity.
- *Publisher*: An entity responsible for making the resource available. Examples of a Publisher include a person, an organization, or a service. Typically, the name of a Publisher should be used to indicate the entity.
- *Source*: A related resource from which the described resource is derived. The described resource may be derived from the related resource in whole or in part. Recommended best practice is to identify the related resource by means of a string conforming to a formal identification system.
- *Relation*: A related resource. Recommended best practice is to identify the related resource by means of a string conforming to a formal identification system.

- *Type:* The nature or genre of the resource. Recommended best practice is to use a controlled vocabulary such as the DCMI Type Vocabulary. To describe the file format, physical medium, or dimensions of the resource, use the Format element.
- *Language*: A language of the resource. Recommended best practice is to use a controlled vocabulary such as RFC 4646.
- *Format*: The file format, physical medium, or dimensions of the resource. Examples of dimensions include size and duration. Recommended best practice is to use a controlled vocabulary such as the list of Internet Media Types.
- *Date*: A point or period of time associated with an event in the life cycle of the resource. Date may be used to express temporal information at any level of granularity. Recommended best practice is to use an encoding scheme, such as the W3CDTF profile of ISO 8601.
- *Rights*: Information about rights held in and over the resource. Typically, rights information includes a statement about various property rights associated with the resource, including intellectual property rights.
- *Identifier*: An unambiguous reference to the resource within a given context. Recommended best practice is to identify the resource by means of a string conforming to a formal identification system.

(from DCMI, 2012, rearranged)

Every element is repeatable, if needed, and is optional, so that greater flexibility than in traditional catalogs can be adopted, according to needs and the assets to hand. For example, a resource can first be indexed with just a title and a date, while for other projects the full list of metadata elements can be applied. In time, optional qualifiers have also been defined for elements, to allow greater expressivity when needed.

As mentioned above, the subject content can be expressed by the Subject and Description elements. Subject can be expressed in many ways, including reference to a standard KOS such as LCSH or DDC – a choice that will further improve the value of metadata information, as it connects it to well-developed and internationally agreed KOSs. Here is an example of the DDC class for spiders expressed as Dublin Core metadata:

```
<meta name='DCTERMS.subject.classification' scheme='DDC'
content='595.44'>.
```

DC metadata can be recorded in a database external to the indexed resources, usually searchable through a web interface and including links to the actual resources; or it can be integrated directly into the HTML (HyperText Markup Language) code of the web page itself, in the *HEAD* section, which is usually not displayed in the content window by web browsers. In this case, it can be exploited by search engines to make the results of their search more precise.

The following are the real DC metadata for the article on 'Facet' in the *ISKO Encyclopedia of Knowledge Organization* (Hudon, 2019).

```
<meta name='DCTERMS.title' content='Facet' />
<meta name='DCTERMS.creator' content='Michele Hudon' />
<meta name='DCTERMS.issued' content='2019' />
<meta name='DCTERMS.relation.ispartof'
      content='ISKO Encyclopedia of Knowledge Organization' />
<meta name='DCTERMS.ispartof'
      content='ISKO Encyclopedia of Knowledge Organization' />
<meta name='DCTERMS:bibliographicCitation'
      content='ISKO Encyclopedia of Knowledge Organization, eds Birger
      Hjorland and Claudio Gnoli' />
<meta name='DCTERMS.subject.classification' scheme='DDC'
      content='001.012'>
<meta name='DCTERMS.subject.classification' scheme='DDC'
      content='025.4'>
<meta name='DCTERMS.subject.keyword' content='facet analysis'>
<meta name='DCTERMS.subject.keyword' content='faceted
      classification'>
<meta name='DCTERMS.subject.keyword' content='S.R. Ranganathan'>
<meta name='DCTERMS.type' content='Text' />
<meta name='DCTERMS.format' content='text/html' />
<meta name='DCTERMS.identifier' content=
      'http://www.isko.org/cyclo/facet' />
```

By the way, *001.012* is a DDC number for 'knowledge organization', built from *001* 'knowledge' and *-012* 'classification'; while *025.4* is 'subject analysis and control' as part of *020* 'library science'.

Similar considerations and functionalities apply for metadata in other formats. These include *microdata*, which specify that a given section or element within a document has a certain nature, e.g. is its title or author. For this purpose, a framework for microdata called *Schema.org* has been developed. For example, in the HTML source code of the same article as above, title is marked by the following microdata.

```
<div itemscope itemtype='http://schema.org/Article'>
<h2 itemprop='headline'>Facet</h2>
</div>
```

5.4 The Semantic Web and linked data

In recent years, it has become common to publish data in standard formats that are meant as contributions to building a Semantic Web.

Data as structured in database fields and records cannot be found directly by a search engine, but requires users to actively formulate a query and examine a set of results. On the other hand, markup languages and formats for the Semantic Web, such as XML and RDF, allow publication of full data directly as web documents that can be visualized and reused by any web user. Such data can be the result of exporting data that was previously in a structured database, or it can be published directly in this form.

The basic principle is similar to that of MARC: instead of filling fixed-length fields like the columns of a large table, any data is optional and, when it occurs, is preceded and followed by a marker that specifies the nature of the data. For example, *spiders* as a subject heading can be written in some XML syntax of this kind:

<subject>spiders</subject>.

XML is an extension of the Standard Generalized Markup Language (SGML). Another application of SGML is the HTML in which most web pages are written:

<p>Subject: spiders</p>.

As can be seen, SGML markers are always written between the < > angle-bracket signs; also, they are repeated at the end of the marked content with the addition of a slash, meaning that this is the closing marker. While HTML provides for only a limited number of markers, such as title, headings *<h1>*, *<h2>* ..., paragraph *<p>* and some text-formatting elements, in XML markers can be defined at will according to the needs on hand, so we have imagined a *<subject>* marker in the example above.

XML syntax also allows the encapsulation of one element inside another, so that constructions like the following are possible:

<document id='12345'>
    <title>An atlas of spiders of the world</title>
    <subject>spiders</subject>
</document>.

This is equivalent to recording the same information in a relational database with a table called *Documents* that includes the fields *id, title* and *subject*. However, this time the information is published on the web in a more explicit (and longer) form.

The adjective *semantic* here refers to the fact that every information element is marked in a meaningful way, for example, the *<title>* marker means that what is enclosed is a title. This contrasts with most HTML elements, which are purely structural and syntactical: *<p>* just means 'paragraph' and gives no clue about the semantic content of the paragraph. One should be careful not to confuse this sense of *semantic* with that used in traditional cataloging, especially in some national traditions, where *semantic indexing* meant 'indexing by subject', so that subject headings and classification numbers were semantic but titles, authors and publishing dates were not (usually being labeled as *descriptive indexing*). The advent of the Semantic Web has introduced some terminological confusion between the two communities, because in the Semantic Web even a title (as in our example above), author or publication date elements can be qualified as 'semantic', as opposed, for example, to a generic paragraph element.

Our example also follows the logic of RDF, the standard specifying that resources are described in the form of *triples* of information, that is, two elements (called the *subject* and the *object*) connected by a *property* (relationship).

In the example above, a triple can be *'12345' hasTitle 'An atlas of spiders of the world'*, where *hasTitle* is a property corresponding to the *<title>* marker in the XML example. RDF data can be expressed with XML syntax or with another syntax, like the simpler Turtle syntax (see section 5.5).

As the same entity can be connected to different entities by different relationships – a book is connected to its title by a title relationship, to its subject by a subject relationship, etc. – sets of an appropriate number of RDF triples can be used to build complex networks of conceptual relationships.

Another important component of linked data is uniform resource identifiers (URI). In our example *spiders* is just a string of characters. But the concept of spiders can also be recorded in a KOS, such as DDC or ILC, that provides a more meaningful reference to spiders, because in the KOS these are part of a complex scheme. To reference a concept in a KOS we need the KOS itself to be published on the internet so that each concept in it can be given a URI. This can be done using formats specific for KOSs, such as SKOS and OWL, which are described in the next section.

5.5 KOSs as linked data

The Semantic Web has been described as a utopian project, because most web content is still published in non-structured ways. We probably should not think of it as an alternative to the existing web, but as a property of the web that can gradually expand. As further explicitly structured data is made available, the web becomes increasingly semantic.

Lately, in the discourse of computer and information science, the focus has shifted from the totality of the web to individual sets of data that are published and can be connected to each other – that is, *linked data*. A dataset may be linked internally, as some data is associated to others (e.g., the subject label *spiders* is associated with several documents in the dataset), and also externally, if several datasets make use of common labels, thus becoming nodes in a potentially worldwide network of data. Clearly, the latter requires that data editors have agreed (even silently, if an existing format is later adopted by another dataset) on the use of common markup languages and element sets. This requirement is called *interoperability* and is clearly not just a technical issue, but also one of KO.

Suppose that you are publishing some bibliographic information on the Semantic Web, including country of publication of each document, marked by a *<country>* element. The content of this element can be only one of some 200 countries existing on the Earth. It may be practical to provide a list of them in advance, from which the indexer can select, e.g., by browsing a drop-down menu. This list may be called a 'controlled vocabulary' by people in computer science, although it is not one in the strict sense of being a structured thesaurus or subject heading list as in the traditional indexing sense described in section 4.4.

Can such full KOSs as thesauri or classification schemes be exploited for linked data? They obviously can, and are even needed if we want to achieve not just technical interoperability but also conceptual interoperability. The data describing the documents owned by two different museums may all be in RDF format, and hence technically interoperable, but they will not be conceptually interoperable if they are based on different schemes.

As we know, standard KOSs used internationally do exist, like the Art and Architecture Thesaurus and the DDC. Therefore, what is needed is simply to express these KOSs in the syntax of linked data. To this purpose, the SKOS model has been developed and approved as a standard by the World Wide Web Consortium (W3C, 2004a).

SKOS is not a very meaningful acronym, as it just means 'Simple KOS'. The term *simple* is appropriate anyway, as SKOS specifies mainly for the basic structural relationships of a thesaurus (BT, NT, RT), with only some attributes for classification schemes. Expressive notation, faceted structures, etc. are not covered in SKOS, so that some of their semantic richness may be lost when expressing a sophisticated KOS in SKOS (Zeng et al., 2010; Gnoli et al., 2011). Still, publishing KOS data in this format is useful because it is a standard, allowing for at least partial interoperability with other semantic data.

Some important KOSs are progressively being published on the web in SKOS format. Unfortunately, DDC is currently not available in this format, possibly due to its commercial management. The second edition of ILC was published in SKOS in 2019 at www.iskoi.org/ilc/skos.php.

The scheme first declares its reference to existing RDF and SKOS specifications, which will be expressed by shortened prefixes in the remaining part of the document:

> *@prefix rdfs: <http://www.w3.org/2000/01/rdf-schema#> .*
> *@prefix skos: <http://www.w3.org/2004/02/skos/core#> .*
> *@prefix ilc2: <http://www.iskoi.org/ilc/2/class/> .*

The name of the KOS is then specified by providing its *label* properties. Also, its nature of concept scheme is specified by the *a* property (an alias of the *rdf:type* property):

> *<http://www.iskoi.org/ilc/2/scheme>*
>   *rdfs:label 'Integrative Levels Classification (ILC)'@en ;*
>   *skos:prefLabel 'Integrative Levels Classification (ILC)'@en ;*
>   *a skos:ConceptScheme .*

The list of all ILC classes follows, each linked to the same relevant properties. Let us take our classes for arachnids and its subclass for spiders as an example:

> *ilc2:mqrd*
> *skos:notation 'mqrd' ;*
> *rdfs:label 'arachnids'@en ;*
> *skos:prefLabel 'arachnids'@en ;*
> *a skos:Concept ;*
> *skos:narrower ilc2:mqrds;*
>
> *ilc2:mqrds*
> *rdfs:seeAlso <http://www.iskoi.org/ilc/2/details.php?no=mqrds> ;*
> *skos:altLabel 'araneae'@en ;*
> *skos:broader ilc2:mqrd ;*
> *skos:notation 'mqrds' ;*
> *rdfs:label 'spiders'@en ;*
> *skos:prefLabel 'spiders'@en ;*
> *skos:inScheme <http://www.iskoi.org/ilc/2/scheme> ;*
> *a skos:Concept .*

If URIs are written in an explicit form, the data looks more complex (only the spiders class is shown):

```
<http://www.iskoi.org/ilc/2/class/mqrds>
       a <http://www.w3.org/2004/02/skos/core#Concept>;
       rdfs:label 'spiders'@en;
       rdfs:seeAlso <http://www.iskoi.org/ilc/2/details.php?no=mqrds>;
       <http://www.w3.org/2004/02/skos/core#altLabel> 'araneae'@en;
       <http://www.w3.org/2004/02/skos/core#broader>
              <http://www.iskoi.org/ilc/2/class/mqrd>;
       <http://www.w3.org/2004/02/skos/core#inScheme>
              <http://www.iskoi.org/ilc/2/scheme>;
       <http://www.w3.org/2004/02/skos/core#notation>
              'mqrds'^^xsd:string;
       <http://www.w3.org/2004/02/skos/core#prefLabel> 'spiders'@en.
```

The subject of all properties is in the first line. It is class *mqrds*, specified as a URI. Each subsequent line introduces a new property. The second line specifies that *mqrds* is a concept, as defined in the SKOS standard. The next line specifies that *mqrds* has a label, which is a string, 'spiders', in the English language. A synonym (*altLabel*) is also available: 'araneae'. Relationship with the parent class *mqrd* is specified by the SKOS *broader* property. And so on.

The last example is given in Turtle, one of the syntactical variants in which RDF data can be expressed. Turtle is relatively easier to understand by the human eye, as the subject of each relationship is shown only in the first line. On the other hand, in the NTriples syntax the subject is repeated for each triple. The same information is then written like this:

```
<http://www.iskoi.org/ilc/2/class/mqrds>
<http://www.w3.org/1999/02/22-rdf-syntax-ns#type>
<http://www.w3.org/2004/02/skos/core#Concept> .

<http://www.iskoi.org/ilc/2/class/mqrds>
<http://www.w3.org/2004/02/skos/core#notation>
'mqrds'^^<http://www.w3.org/2001/XMLSchema#string> .

<http://www.iskoi.org/ilc/2/class/mqrds>
<http://www.w3.org/2004/02/skos/core#inScheme>
<http://www.iskoi.org/ilc/2/scheme> .

<http://www.iskoi.org/ilc/2/class/mqrds>
<http://www.w3.org/2000/01/rdf-schema#label>
'spiders'@en .
```

```
<http://www.iskoi.org/ilc/2/class/mqrds>
<http://www.w3.org/2004/02/skos/core#prefLabel>
'spiders'@en .
```

```
<http://www.iskoi.org/ilc/2/class/mqrds>
<http://www.w3.org/2004/02/skos/core#altLabel>
'araneae'@en .
```

```
<http://www.iskoi.org/ilc/2/class/mqrds>
<http://www.w3.org/2004/02/skos/core#broader>
<http://www.iskoi.org/ilc/2/class/mqrd> .
```

While SKOS allows for expressing the structure of a thesaurus and, with some limitations, a classification scheme, the structure of an ontology including many relationships, logical restrictions and rules is much more complex and cannot be expressed in SKOS. For this purpose, a more general standard is available, the Web Ontology Language (OWL). Reflecting the complexity of ontologies, OWL is composed of many elements and is best managed with specific editing tools that can readily provide the needed elements in the appropriate syntax.

The following is a simple excerpt of an example ontology expressed in OWL (W3C, 2004b) for a class of wine:

```
<owl:Class rdf:ID='Wine'>
        <rdfs:label xml:lang='en'>wine</rdfs:label>
        <rdfs:label xml:lang='fr'>vin</rdfs:label>
        <rdfs:subClassOf rdf:resource='&food;PotableLiquid'/>
        <rdfs:subClassOf>
                <owl:Restriction>
                        <owl:onProperty rdf:resource='#madeFromGrape'/>
                        <owl:minCardinality rdf:datatype= '&xsd;non
                                NegativeInteger'>1</owl:minCardinality>
                </owl:Restriction>
        </rdfs:subClassOf>
        ...
</owl:Class>.
```

Properties can also be defined:

```
<owl:ObjectProperty rdf:ID='madeFromGrape'>
        <rdfs:domain rdf:resource='#Wine'/>
        <rdfs:range rdf:resource='#WineGrape'/>
</owl:ObjectProperty>.
```

As can be seen, standards such as SKOS and OWL allow the network of concepts and relationships of a KOS that we saw in Chapters 3 and 4 to be represented in formal, machine-readable ways.

CHAPTER 6

Applying knowledge organization

6.1 Organizing phenomena

In this final chapter we will consider how the principles and techniques of KO can be applied in practice to the variety of knowledge resources. We start again with the first dimension of knowledge that is relevant to KO: classes of phenomena.

One simple need of human knowledge is to organize its objects into manageable groups, to be discussed and further examined. In all sciences an important component is what is variously called 'systematics', 'taxonomy' or 'classification' of the phenomena studied. In our review of KOS types we saw that the term *taxonomies* is often adopted for hierarchical systems of objects, such as plants, wines or cars, as distinguished from systems of document subjects (see section 4.4.2).

For example, systematic biology is the branch of biology dealing with the ordering, listing and nomenclature of the different kinds of organisms. Systematic biology produces hierarchical KOSs of animals, plants, fungi, etc. that are biological taxonomies. The term *classification* in this field is usually reserved to the act of identifying the species and the higher groups (*taxa*) to which a specimen belongs by inspecting its relevant characters (say, shape of leaves, number and color of petals, etc.) and comparing them with those of groups known in the literature.

Systematics often develops quite early in the history of a science. After some general description, the variety of objects needs to be organized at least in some provisional way in order to get a picture of the field. While animals and plants were already described by simple lists in antiquity, such phenomena as climates, soils or languages have started to be systematized only relatively recently. This is because such objects are more complex and need a greater effort to be defined, identified and compared: for example, while a giraffe is clearly different from an antelope, the dialects of Occitan are articulated systems of spoken sounds that need long research before being described and distinguished from those of Catalan (systematic work in linguistics is known as 'typology').

As work proceeds, groups of languages may be identified as part of more general categories, such as Romance languages, in turn grouped in Indo-European languages and so on: in this way a hierarchy of classes and subclasses is developed. Like any KOS, scientific taxonomies can always be revised and updated, so that, for example, a European language like Basque is acknowledged to have such different characters from its geographical neighbors as to have been moved outside the Indo-European family.

It is in the very nature of scientific research that systems of knowledge are open to criticism and revision, hence KOSs change accordingly. This may cause some practical drawbacks, as certain museums, manuals, etc. may still be adopting older taxonomies and nomenclatures, and their users may need more inertial time to learn and apply the new organization.

Also, different schools may adopt different criteria by which to organize phenomena. A major alternative is always that between morphological characters and genealogical history (Gnoli, 2018a): while *phenetic* systematists give priority to the former, thus concluding that birds are a class separate from reptiles because of their obvious structural differences (feathers, wings, hollow bones, etc.), *cladistic* systematists give priority to the latter, concluding that birds are a subclass of reptiles because they originated in a secondary branch of the reptiles tree. This results in the two schools producing different taxonomies and nomenclatures.

Despite being always subject to revision, systematic accounts are an essential starting point in the development of any science. Only once we have a scheme of the studied objects can we refer to them in clear ways, compare them, collect new observations and data about them and develop new insights and deeper theories as a consequence. In other words, KO is an essential part of science.

Another application of KO principles is the arrangement of the broadest classes of phenomena, and of the corresponding sciences, into a general scheme of the whole of knowledge. As we saw in section 1.4, the classification of the sciences has been a classic problem, confronted by many philosophers in every age. If we consider the phenomena themselves, independently from our methods of studying them (that is, if we take an ontological approach as opposed to an epistemological one: see section 2.4.5), we can identify what have been called integrative levels, and arrange the sciences according to their sequence of increasing organization, as done by Comte, Bliss and other modern authors:

matter (physics)
life (biology)
mind (psychology)
society (social sciences)
culture (humanities).

A commonly discussed issue is where to place the abstract sciences of mathematics and logic in this scheme (Fraser, 2019). Some claim that they are a product of the human intellect, which would imply that they be listed at the end. On the other hand, a Platonist approach assumes that these disciplines study something that exists independently of our knowledge, that is, that the universe is mathematical in itself: this will result in their placement at the beginning of the list (a solution adopted more commonly, e.g. by Bliss, Colon and the ILC).

These major levels can be further analyzed into minor ones. The classic example is that of biology, which can easily be divided into branches studying objects of increasing organization:

genes (genetics)
cells (cytology)
tissues (histology)
organs (anatomy or morphology)
organisms (botany, zoology, etc.)
populations (population biology)
ecosystems (ecology).

While level analysis is an important methodological tool, not all divisions follow this principle. Indeed, certain scientific branches are defined by their methods rather than their objects (that is, by epistemological rather than ontological principles), giving rise to classes that are orthogonal to those above. Think of evolutionary biology, which is the study of life in its historical aspect, so that it can combine with any level to give evolutionary genetics, evolutionary botany, etc.

The same is true at the broader rank of all the sciences: history is the study of any phenomenon in its chronological aspects, so that there is a history of life, a history of society and a history of culture. Mills and Broughton (1977, 36–7) mention science, philosophy, history and art as 'fundamental disciplines' or 'forms of knowledge' defined in epistemological terms, as opposed to their 'sub-disciplines' identified by the phenomena studied (science of language, philosophy of language and so on).

Other principles can also be invoked. For example, the philosopher Charles S. Peirce divided all sciences by applying his categories of 'firstness', 'secondness' and 'thirdness' recursively, resulting in a very original tree with ternary branches.

6.2 Organizing educational and reference content

The organization of phenomena has obvious consequences for the way their knowledge is transmitted in education. The structure of educational materials has to conform somehow to the relationships that have been identified between different classes of phenomena: if organisms have been found to be made of cells, then the study of organisms and the study of cells have to be related in a biology textbook.

However, this does not mean that phenomena must necessarily be studied in the order of their levels. Classes and textbooks may also start with whole organisms, as they are the phenomena perceived most immediately, and then continue on to their microscopic components in separate modules. What is important is that the relationships between these phenomena are made clear in the structure of learning materials.

This kind of organization can be implemented in the very structure of volumes, chapters and sections, as is seen in tables of contents (TOC). Well-designed TOCs are effective syntheses of works and the relationships between their parts. Section headings and subheadings may be discursive and 'friendly', or use precise and technical terms, making the TOC itself a sort of thesaurus.

The numbering of sections (*2.5*, *2.5.1*, ...) may provide a meaningful hierarchical structure. Ranganathan applied his principles for notation even to the section numbering of his books, and articulated their text in many small sections, so that, for example, section *VC21* 'Separation in Call Number' is part of section *VC2* 'Distinctiveness in Call Number', belonging to chapter *VC* 'Call Number', which in turn belongs to part *V* 'Use of Collection Number' (Ranganathan, 1967). Referring to section *VC21* rather than to page 520 is then much more precise, as the structure of the section number contains information about its content, which will not change if, for example, the same work is republished in a digital edition. Such practices may look like the professional obsession of a classificationist; but they provide additional guides to the exploration and discussion of a subject, at the same time providing an immediate example of application of classification techniques to a real case.

Another concrete application of KO in educational material is synthetic schemes and diagrams that illustrate connections between the parts discussed in each section. Chronological schemes may help in understanding which phenomena were contemporary with each other, hence possibly related, such as the introduction of triennial rotation in agriculture and an increase of population in demography. Graphics and visualization thus play a very important role in KO.

The organization of content is even more prominent in reference works, such as encyclopedias of a special domain or of the whole of knowledge. While alphabetical order may be a practical solution for browsing, encyclopedias often include synoptic views of certain topics, working as additional guides to the exploration of individual entries. Think of 'portals' in Wikipedia that introduce a domain with a general, synthetic treatment, containing many links to specific entries. This is not fundamentally different from the famous 18th-century *Encyclopédie*: the latter included a classification scheme of all the sciences and many cross-references from one entry to others, all together forming a semantic network that virtually defined a KOS, as illustrated in the excerpt from Diderot (1755) quoted in section 1.3.

The very word *encyclop(a)edia* comes from Greek terms meaning a teaching, especially for children (*paidéia*), which is organized in a circular way (*en-kýklios*), as all subjects were thought of as interrelated in ways that could be followed along a path, eventually coming back to the starting point. That is, no information should be taken as isolated: all knowledge is connected, and what help us to realize this and to see knowledge as a whole are KOSs.

From the same Greek stem comes *pedagogy*, the technique of teaching that studies how knowledge can be best transmitted and learned. Jean Piaget, a master of pedagogy, was very interested in how children organize new knowledge in their minds by constructing *schemata* (Piaget, 1953).

Educational applications of KO are often cited in the work of Dagobert Soergel (2015), another prominent author, emphasizing that information resources, especially educational ones, should be organized primarily with their end users in mind (section 2.4.1): 'meaningful or deep learning can be supported through well-structured presentation of material, through giving learners schemas they can use to organize knowledge in their minds, and through helping learners to understand knowledge organization principles they can use to construct their own schemas' (Soergel, 2014, 22).

The complexity of knowledge makes some parts of it necessary in order to understand other parts, due both to actual relationships between the phenomena studied and to the dynamics of knowledge acquisition processes. The more basic topics are said to be *pro-paedeutical* (preparatory) for more advanced ones.

This has consequences for the sequence in which subjects have to be taught in college and university curricula. Engineering students need to learn mathematical calculus before they are able to study the physics of solid bodies; this in turn is a basis for the design of stable structures, such as buildings or bridges, and their architecture. Although new students may be more attracted by the creative aspects of these final applications, they first need to master differential equations! The same is true for aspiring botanists dreaming of the study of life in the field, who in their first years have to wrestle with formulas and reactions in organic chemistry.

Therefore, another important application of KO is the design and management of learning curricula. This includes the way subjects are distributed across different classes and examinations, the optimal number of hours to be devoted to each module, the naming of learning units, classes, degrees and doctoral schools.

Similar considerations may relate to the subjects dealt with by an institution or a government. The names and hierarchies of offices and departments are another kind of KOS, oriented towards action rather than teaching or writing. A good example are the lists of departments and their ministers, which are not fixed but may be established by each individual government. For example, in Western countries it is common to find a department of Economic Development, but not one of Personal Development. The perspective changes when we look at such governments as that of Bhutan, which includes a Department of Traditional Medicine, or Saudi Arabia, which includes a Committee for the Promotion of Virtue and the Prevention of Vice. Institutional KOSs clearly reveal the political and cultural assumptions behind the formality of administrative work.

6.3 Indexing documents

As knowledge in our society is handled in the form of documents, organizing knowledge most often takes the form of examining such documents and recording their subject contents so that they can be related to other documents in networks of available knowledge assets.

We saw in section 2.4.3 that documents can consist in many different objects, from a compact disc, to a book, to an antelope in a zoo. Although their external and material forms can also be described and searched in an index (looking for color images, for documents in the French language, etc.), the core object of KO is subject content.

Content is typically expressed in the form of some text: while pictorial, audiovisual or material documents are also important cases (see section 6.3.4), they are often described in textual captions, such as the title of a painting or the synopsis of a movie, because text is the most typical way of recording and exchanging knowledge in our civilization. Therefore, the organization of document content typically consists in the analysis and summarization of texts.

A deep approach to indexing aims at representing all subjects mentioned in a text. This can be useful for producing a subject index of the text, especially in such cases as academic monographs or handbooks. This kind of index is often published at the end of the text itself, using keywords arranged alphabetically. In some cases a single keyword can work as a main access point, under which more specific subheadings are listed, thus combining alphabetical and systematic ordering. A real example from Golub (2015) is:

> *ontologies*:
>> *definition*, 23, 59–60
>> *mappings of*, 69–70
>> *Open Biological and Biomedical Ontologies (OBO)*, 86–7
>> *standards for*, 85–7
>> see also *knowledge organization system (KOS)-ontologies*
>>> *Web Ontology Language (OWL)*, 85–7.

Back-of-the-book indexes require their compilers to read the whole text carefully. Indexes may be produced by the authors themselves, or by private professionals who are paid for this time-consuming activity. In some countries they are organized in professional associations of *indexers* and are connected through such specialized journals as *The Indexer: the International Journal of Indexing*.

Which subjects should be chosen for a back-of-the-book index, and by what terms should they be expressed? Although keyword choice is free, just as in the case of tags, good practices and principles do exist and experience in this job is valuable. Some principles of morphology, stemming, etc. that are common to thesauri can be applied: in the example above, the plural form *ontologies* has been adopted rather than the singular *ontology*; acronyms are always cited in brackets after the full form; and so on.

A similar procedure is often adopted to produce the keyword sets for a scientific paper, or the tag sets for a blog post or a video shared on the internet. In these cases, however, the set is much more limited, as it may consist of just five to ten keywords. This means that there is no need to order them alphabetically, although this may still be the most reasonable way to determine their order. In the case of folksonomies, as we know, the consistency of tag selection and form is often limited as a result of the dynamics of any open system. In the case of scientific papers, some publishers may require authors to select keywords from a vocabulary of already used ones, or possibly to propose the addition of some new ones. This light form of vocabulary control should produce better consistency across different papers.

If one is dealing with a collection of longer texts, such as monographs, indexing has to be more synthetic, as no cataloger has the time to read the whole of each document they are indexing. The themes discussed in the text have to be ascertained by a general examination of the item to hand: its title, subtitle, table of contents and structure, abstract if available, preface, chapter headings, commercial presentation, etc. An experienced cataloger will usually be able to identify relevant themes in a reliable way, and to express them appropriately in an indexing language.

These processes of content analysis are not easily formalized, and there will always be an element of subjectivity. Studies have been conducted to assess *inter-indexer consistency*, often showing that different indexers choose different terms or classes for the same text. Consistency in subject representation is an ideal to which indexers try to approximate, rather than an absolute result. Also, they can be biased by the particular purposes of the collection they are organizing (see section 6.4).

Despite these subjective components, a standard model of the procedures involved in content analysis may be of help in identifying some reference principles, as illustrated in the next section.

6.3.1 Content analysis

Let us consider an individual text, like a monograph in any printed or digital form. It consists of words and is structured in parts, chapters and sections. This is also called the *macrostructure* of the text. Specific points can also be identified by page numbers – a parameter originating from the format of printed books that is still retained, conventionally, in many digital documents.

So, we may wonder what the whole text is about and what its individual components are about. A text often has a main argument or thesis, which we called its base theme in section 3.6.1. While developing the base theme through the text, the authors can gradually introduce related arguments and facts, which are particular themes. This macrostructure can be ideally represented in a simple scheme that provides a first step towards its representation in the *microstructure* of a subject heading or a classmark.

To this end, recommendations are provided by ISO 5963:1985 *Documentation – Methods for examining documents, determining their subjects, and selecting indexing terms* (available to purchase at https://www.iso.org/obp/ui/#iso:std:iso: 5963:ed-1:v1:en). After some definitions and advice concerning the meaningful elements to be considered in a document, the standard indicates that the indexer should consider the main elements discussed in it, in terms of relationships between them:

- Does the subject include a concept denoting an activity (e.g. an action, an operation, a process, etc.)?
- Is the activity discussed in the document performed on any particular subject?
- Does the object undergo the identified activity?
- Does the document debate the agent of this action?
- Does it concern any particular means to do the action (for example any special tools, techniques or methods)?
- Is any dependent or independent variable identified?
- Has the subject been considered under any particular viewpoint usually not associated to that research domain?

As can be seen, this procedure is reminiscent of the categories of facet analysis – action, agent, instrument, etc. (see section 3.5.1). With its guidance, indexers should be able to identify the set of themes that are discussed in a document and to assess the linkages between them.

Cheti (1996) provides an example of the thematic organization of a text, Guy Aznar's 1993 French book *Travailler moins pour travailler tous: 20 propositions* (Working less so that all can work: 20 proposals). He identifies a sequence and interconnection of themes (*T*) and rhemes (*R*, see section 3.6.3) in the text:

- Unemployment (T1) cannot be eliminated nor significantly reduced through the following strategies (R1): an increase of economic growth (R1a), a reduction of productivity (R1b).
- Economic growth (T2=R1a), whether it occurred, would not create more occupation (R2).
- Reduction of productivity (T3=R1b) is an unrealistic objective (R3).
- Unemployment (T1) can be eliminated through apportionment of work (R4).
- Apportionment of work (T4=R4) can be achieved through the following strategies (R5): reducing collective work time (R5a), division of unemployment (R5b), choosing part-time work (R5c).
- Reduction of collective work time (T5=R5a) consists in ... (R6).
- Division of unemployment (T6=R5b) consists in ... (R7).
- Part-time work (T7=R5c) may consist in the following forms (R8): classic half-time (R8a), parental half-time (R8b), qualification half-time (R8c), etc.
- Classic half-time (T8=R8a) consists in ... (R9).
- Parental half-time (T9=R8b) consists in ... (R10).
- Qualification half-time (T10=R8c) consists in the possibility of moving from full-time to half-time to attend a training course (R11).
- Apportionment of work (T4) is also aimed at increasing spare time (R12).
- Spare time (T11=R12) is ... (R13).

Of these, some themes (T1, T4) work as macrothemes, that is, dominant themes, giving unity to subordinated themes. For example, T10, T9, T8 are subordinated to T7, inasmuch as they are means through which part-time is implemented; T7 is subordinated to T4, inasmuch as it is one of the strategies through which apportionment of work is implemented. One can say, then, that the propositions having T10, T9, T8 as their themes specify T7, and the proposition having T7 as its theme specifies T4.

Finally, T4 appears to be the dominant subject in the whole text, as the proposition T4–R5 is implied by the propositions T1–R4 and T4–R12. That is, the propositions 'unemployment can be reduced through apportionment of work' (A) and 'is also aimed at increasing spare time' (B) imply the proposition 'apportionment of work consists in working less so that everybody can work' (C); in other words, from C follow A and B.

So, T4 can be chosen as the base theme, and other particular themes can be expressed in relation to it. Other particular themes may be suppressed according to the required degree of detail (see next section).

6.3.2 Content expression

The expression of content can be done by free keywords and tags, or by some controlled vocabulary, or by a notation – the different KOS types that were reviewed in Chapter 4. However, the basic principles and rules of content analysis will remain the same.

As we saw in section 3.6.2, free and freely-faceted systems enable the representation of particular themes as connected to the base theme, which should be cited first in order to determine the position of the document in the main sequence, e.g. in the arrangement on the shelves or in the display of search results. A document in which crustaceans are the main theme, with conservation and ships as particular themes, can be indexed like this:

> *mqrh ve wvlh* crustaceans; conservation; ships.

From particular themes, cross-references may be provided in the index, of the kind known as *chain indexing* in the time of printed catalogs:

> *ve* conservation
> > see also *mqrh ve wvlh* crustaceans; conservation; ships
>
> ...
>
> *wvlh* ships
> > see also *mqrh ve wvlh* crustaceans; conservation; ships.

Nowadays this function is easily provided by digital catalogs, which can find a string (like *ve*) in whatever position within a heading, rather than by just scanning the index in alphabetical order as a human does. Still, systematic order is useful for organizing the search results in a clear way for cognitive purposes. This can be observed in the following example of subjects involving conservation (*ve*) as a particular theme associated to different main themes:

mq ve	animals; conservation
mqrh ve wvlh	crustaceans; conservation; ships
tad ve	crimes; conservation
tay ve	regulations; conservation
ve	conservation
vey	landscape management
yiyr ve	moral philosophy; conservation.

In these examples, themes are always combined in a *post-coordinate way*; that is, they are simply listed (although in a specific citation order, where the base theme is cited at the beginning of the string). Keywords and tags in scientific papers and blogs are other examples of post-coordinate indexing. The task of retrieving meaningful elements is left to the search mechanism and the relationships between them are not specified (although some can be guessed by the user examining the strings: 'regulations; conservation' will likely refer to regulations concerning conservation, rather than to conservation of regulations).

Alternatively, relationships between themes can be specified in a *pre-coordinate* way, as in our freely-faceted examples from section 3.6.2:

mqrh0wvlh	crustaceans, as related (in general) to ships
mqrh2wvlh	crustaceans, in/on ships
mqrh3wvlh	crustaceans, affected by ships
mqrh4wvlh	crustaceans, disturbed by ships;

mqrh53ve4wvlh	crustaceans, undergoing conservation, disturbed by ships.

As we have mentioned, indexers have to decide whether each theme is worth being expressed or not. This also depends on the detail required in the index and its intended size: while back-of-the-book indexes and scientific paper keywords should represent all particular themes, a library catalog will be able to organize books by basic themes, and only a selection of particular themes can be expressed as their facets.

Although one might believe that careful representation of particular themes is always an advantage, it is not necessarily so. Ideally, any word in a text can be an access point (as happens in automatic indexing of full texts, see next section), but then each document will be related to an exceedingly vast set of concepts.

In practice, a theme that is mentioned only incidentally in a text will not be a good access point. Imagine that ships are cited in a section of text only as an example of crustaceans' interaction with human activities, but none of the rest of the text deals with ships. If ships are cited in the subject string a user looking for information on ships will retrieve this document, probably together with many others where ships are mentioned only incidentally. But their search will then be quite noisy, and will not enable them to identify the most relevant documents from where their research should start. In other words, although the *recall* of the search will be good – that is, many documents related to ships will be found – its *precision* will be poor, as many of the documents retrieved will not be really focused on the selected concept – they will not really focus on ships.

Recall and precision are the two fundamental parameters in information retrieval. Recall can be described as the fraction of potentially relevant available documents, waiting in the depths of a knowledge base, that are actually retrieved in a search. Precision, on the other hand, is the fraction of all retrieved documents that are indeed relevant to the user's search.

Ideally, both recall and precision should be maximized: users wish to find all available relevant documents, and not to have them mixed with irrelevant ones. However, a basic law of information retrieval is that any strategy that increases precision will tend to diminish recall, and vice versa. In other words, the real world is not a searcher's paradise!

Strategies may be implemented either on the searcher side or on the indexer side. As any user of Google web search will have learned, searching for too-common words will result in low precision, but searching for too-specific combinations of words will result in low recall, even zero results. So, each search has to be tuned, including through feedback from some initial attempts, until the optimal degree of specificity is obtained.

Precision and recall are less commonly considered from the viewpoint of the indexer. As we can now understand, indexing policies will affect precision and recall. Indexing in a very deep way, including many particular themes in a subject string, will result in high recall but low precision; on the other hand, selecting only the really important themes will result in low recall and high precision. An optimal balance has to be found in this task, too.

Particular themes can be used to specify the subject of a text, thinking of them as subdivisions of the base theme (crustaceans related to ships are a 'type' of crustaceans in general). This means that, within a set of documents indexed by consistent criteria, documents indexed with a small number of themes should be more general (e.g. a treatise on crustaceans can be indexed by the only theme, *crustaceans*) than those with many themes expressed (crustaceans, in relation to conservation, and to ships, etc.).

Statistically, the latter will be retrieved in a greater number of searches (both when searching for *crustaceans* and when searching for *ships*) than will the former (only when searching for *crustaceans*). This is paradoxical in a way, because general documents should be the main reference search results, as users should start by reading the fundamental treatises before delving into particular aspects of the subject. Therefore, one should not go overboard in expressing particular themes and should try to express a number of themes proportionally to their actual relevance in the text, as compared to other texts one is indexing in the same collection.

Cheti (1996) suggests that the expression of a theme can be determined, besides by the properties of the text itself, by the expected needs of users. This is indeed a reasonable principle in applying indexing to a local situation. However, we also have to consider that in a globalized world data circulates and will reach unexpected new users. The subject of a book in a small library may be shared in online catalogs, converted to linked open data, and one day found by a searcher in the other side of the world, who could discover a relationship relevant to her research in only that book. In such an open world, it is more difficult to foresee which themes might be relevant to users and which ones might not. This argument suggests that indexers should try to adopt standard policies, rather than conform to a particular expected audience.

Another solution for finding a compromise between precision and recall is to transfer a part of the relevant relationships to the KOS used for searching. A text discussing ships will probably also mention the sea on which they sail. However, the relationship between ships and sea or fresh water is true for all ships, not just for particular texts. The KOS can then include this *paradigmatic* relationship as a RT:

wvlh ships $<<$ *jy* seas.

A user browsing the KOS will then be able to remark this relationship and autonomously decide whether an additional search for 'seas' is worthwhile for their particular needs. (This expanded search can be automated in such digital applications as SciGator, see section 6.5.3.) Only for texts that are really focused on the role of the sea as a local context for ships will a *syntagmatic* relationship also be expressed in the particular subject string:

wvlh2jy   ships, in seas.

6.3.3 Automatic methods

The increasing number of documents produced in our digital era makes it hard to apply such careful analysis of content to all of them. This has been a major stimulus in the development of automatic methods of indexing (Golub, 2017).

The basic units available for automatic indexing of texts are words (section 3.1). The longer a text is, the more words it contains that offer potential information about its subject. Such simple titles as 'Difficult times' for a newspaper editorial, or *The Name of the Rose* for a historical novel, can hardly be treated effectively in automatic ways: it would probably not be appropriate to establish by an automatic method that they are, respectively, about *chronology* and *gardening*.

On the other hand, because long texts have many thousands of words some of those words have to be selected as the most meaningful for indexing – that is, they have to be selected as keywords (see section 4.4.1).

A very simple principle is that if a word occurs many times in a text, it is probably more representative of it than words occurring only one or a few times. By automatic means it is easy to produce a list of words arranged by frequency of occurrence in a text (a parameter known as *TF, term frequency*). However, such a list from any English text will probably start with articles, prepositions, conjunctions and pronouns as such 'the', 'of', 'and', 'she', etc. Not usually being relevant for indexing, these can be provided in a separate list of *stopwords*, to be matched with the first list and discarded from it by the indexing algorithm. Of the remaining meaningful words, like 'ship' or 'sea', the most frequent ones will be good candidates to represent the subject content of the document.

Although this method has a sound basis it can still produce quite generic results. Although not as common as 'the' or 'and', a word like 'ship' is also relatively common. This can result in many documents indexed as *ship(s)*, some of which mention ships only as a particular theme that is not very useful in most searches. On the other hand, words like 'crustacean' are less common, so that their occurrence in a text is more likely to represent its content in a specific way. The fact of being an uncommon word can be quantified as the *inverse document frequency (IDF)*: if the frequency of a word is low, say one occurrence in 100,000 words, then its IDF will be high, being equal to 100,000.

Already in 1972, researcher Karen Spärck Jones had the idea of associating term frequency and inverse document frequency in a simple formula so as to assign a numerical value to the relevance of each word in a text. Word relevance could be calculated as the *TF/IDF* ratio (Spärck Jones, 1972). In other words, the relevance of a word increases with its frequency in the text, but also decreases with its general frequency (which can be established from a large-enough corpus of sample texts). If both 'ship(s)' and 'crustacean(s)' occur 15 times in a text, but 'crustacean(s)' is less common overall, its *TD/IDF* value will be higher, hence it will be a better keyword than 'ship(s)'.

This simple formula is still basic in most algorithms for automatic indexing, together with many other specific calculations that have been developed and tested in later approaches and applications.

Of course, machines are unable to understand the meaning of a word, phrase or sentence in the way that humans do. To them, there is no difference in principle among 'bank' at the border of a river, 'bank' as a small hill and 'bank' as a financial institution. However, as in the case of humans, context can help. Another word occurring in the same text may be 'money'. The indexing algorithm can be coupled with a thesaurus where *money* is much closer to *bank* in the third sense than in the others, and the algorithm can be instructed to decide on this basis that a likely category for the text is *banking* in economics.

Effective systems of automatic indexing are often coupled with thesauri or other KOS resources. This point is very instructive as an answer to those claiming that, with the progress of digital technologies, concept-based KO will no longer be relevant. In fact, what is happening is that KOSs are becoming even more relevant, as they can be combined with automatic methods, besides being used directly by human indexers. Intellectual and automatic methods should be seen as complementary, rather than competing.

The research field studying methods of processing words from digital texts for various purposes, including automatic indexing, is called *natural language processing (NLP)*: nowadays, decades after the simple formulas like *TF/IDF*, it is much developed. As its name suggests, it relates to linguistics as well as to computer science (especially its branch of *artificial intelligence, AI*) and KO. NLP and KO are more often associated in certain research traditions and countries, e.g. France, than in others, where KO used to be considered a matter of intellectual analysis and cultural history. Clearly, all these components are relevant in various ways to the task of providing access to knowledge sources by subject.

6.3.4 Non-textual documents

We have assumed until now that our documents consist of text, made up of separate words. However, in section 2.4.3 we also made clear that by *documents* we mean not only texts, but any resource that can be used as a source of knowledge, including pictures, videos, audio recordings, concrete objects kept in museums or animals in a zoo, etc. The techniques of text analysis cannot be applied to these directly.

Although we will not deal with this topic in detail we can mention that there are two basic strategies for dealing with indexing of non-textual documents. The first relies on the fact that such documents, although not texts themselves, are often associated with texts that describe them. A picture can have a title or textual tags, a video can have a description of its content, an animal can have a sign illustrating its name and information on its provenance, habits, etc. In other words, the indexing process can take place in two steps: first the knowledge content is described, via intellectual means, by some human indexer, and then the textual representation can be treated – including digitally and automatically – by some retrieval system.

The second strategy is more difficult but more substantial: the content is analyzed in its specific form as such. For example, a picture is analyzed as to the patterns and colors it contains, and compared with reference rules so as to establish that, for example, it represents a human face, or a car. This information can be stored in a database that is later searched by some digital interface. Research in such techniques of *multimedia information retrieval* (MMIR) is newer, and its achievements are therefore comparatively less advanced than those of text retrieval.

In recent years more manuals have become available (Raieli, 2013) and there are regular events, like ACM's international MMIR conference or IEEE's international conference on Multimedia Information Processing and Retrieval. There is clearly much room for significant progress in this branch of KO.

6.4 Organizing collections

We have seen how the basic principles for the analysis of content are common to all kinds of document, especially if we focus on the phenomena that are discussed: articles on crustaceans, archive records of crustaceans detected by official surveys, photographic or video images of crustaceans, alcohol-fixed crustaceans in a museum or living crustaceans in an aquarium all are sources of knowledge about crustaceans (Gnoli, 2010). At the same time, the different kinds of collection are also a component of KO, as we saw in section 2.4.2. And KO applications obviously change according to the collection context.

A classic application is to bibliographies and directories, which collect only synthetic descriptions of resources such as papers, monographs, also websites and other electronic documents. These descriptions are usually in standardized formats, including basic information such as authors or creators, title, publication date and format. These are completed with subject information, such as subject headings or classmarks.

It is important that this subject part is searchable through bibliographic access points – just as are the authors, title or format – rather than being offered only as a supplementary description. That is, printed directories need to include an alphabetical or notational arrangement that can be browsed, and digital ones need to include search fields and browsable lists for subject content (see section 6.5). Search should be possible both by base theme and by particular themes, and results should be organized accordingly, with documents having the searched-for category as their base theme displayed before those where it is just a particular theme.

Bibliographies specializing in a domain, e.g. mathematics, electrical engineering or psychology, are often provided by private companies in the form of password-regulated access to online databases. General databases of academic literature also exist, such as Web of Science, Scopus and Google Scholar, as well as bibliographies specializing in some cultural areas, e.g. Japanese or Arabic literature (Araújo et al., 2019). These often index their records by ad hoc systems of broad disciplinary categories and subcategories, rather than by international classification systems.

Some special bibliographies have also developed their own KOSs, usually with much greater detail than in general systems, and these have often become international references for those fields. Such is the case of AMS Mathematics Subject Classification, used for many decades to index mathematics literature in what is now the MathSciNet database (Fraser, 2019); or of the system of *Journal of Economic Literature*, also used to organize libraries specializing in economics. Keywords assigned to the papers in the original journal may also be reported in bibliographic records, and serve as additional access points together with words in titles and abstracts.

In libraries, the primary need is to organize books and other documents in rooms and on shelves. As libraries have existed since ancient times their needs have always been a driving force in the development of KOSs (Dousa, 2018), as we saw in section 1.4. If the arrangement of documents in a library is designed from the beginning according to some KOS, the space of the library becomes a physical instantiation of that organization of knowledge and users can walk through the building as if they were surfing knowledge itself. An old example is the Kremsmünster abbey library in Austria: an imposing 17th-century building with as many as seven floors. While the lower floors house books on 'earthly' subjects, such as paleontology and geology, the next ones house increasingly 'higher' subjects, culminating in religion and theology at the top! A similar idea was adopted by the famous architect Renzo Piano for the MuSe Science Museum in Trento, open since 2013, where the terrace and top floors are devoted to the sun and glaciers.

Such architectural designs, sometimes also implementing more recent systems of knowledge, are not just evocative metaphors but a real cognitive aid that promotes exploration and mental associations in a very natural way. The place of a book is not just a neutral address where it can be found in a mechanical way after checking its shelfmark in a catalog: it becomes a hint as to its place in the whole of knowledge and to its connections with books on related subjects. Signs on and near shelves should visualize knowledge context in effective ways (Fabbrizzi, 2014).

We have seen (sections 3.3.1; 3.5.2; 4.4.5) how a well-designed notation can produce meaningful orders, with general topics preceding their own specializations by facets and subclasses of increasing specificity. Ranganathan's Colon Classification also has special 'anteriorizing common isolates' that place introductory surveys and bibliographies on a topic before the plain illustration of the same topic, so that a user can browse the shelf, starting with reference works before delving into the subject, and then into its particular facets. The Indian master called the resulting model *APUPA* (alien-penumbral-umbral-penumbral-alien), meaning that a user looking for a particular topic will find books focusing on the topic in an *umbral* region, surrounded on both sides by books on similar and related topics (*penumbral*), gradually blending into unrelated topics (*alien*) (Bianchini et al., 2017). Indeed, he conceived arrangement on the shelves as the most immediate guide for users, even before searching the catalog – a tool that not all small libraries could afford to produce.

Still today, when rich online catalogs are often available, experience shows that many users prefer to look directly on the shelves. Therefore, the physical arrangement of books according to a good classification is crucial to offering productive and creative paths across knowledge. Of course, library catalogs can provide additional access points, by authors and titles, as well as cross-references by different facets that are not covered in the uni-dimensional linear arrangement of books on shelves.

KOSs, especially controlled vocabularies, can also be applied to the management of records in archives, and archival science has several points of contact with KO (Bragato Barros, 2019). Here, however, organization by subject coexists with the principle of provenance, which states that documents should be kept in an order which follows that of the sources that have produced them (Tognoli and Guimarães, 2018). Thus, for example, the archive of a public institution will be organized according to the different departments and offices that have produced letters and other documents over time. This is still a form of KO, as departments and offices are usually devoted to specific functions and subjects (see section 6.2). Additionally, indexes by specific topic, when resources allow their production and maintenance, can be very useful for discovering recent or historical information on a subject across different institutional sources.

Museums organize artworks and specimens of various material shapes and sizes, rather than printed documents that all have more or less the same shape and size. This means that arrangement in museum spaces is constrained by physical form: a complete whale skeleton may need a whole room, perhaps hanging from the ceiling by some means, while specimens of medium-sized species can be shown in display cases and insect specimens can be arranged in small boxes, to suggest easy comparison of many variants.

Despite such physical constraints, museum rooms, display cases and signs can be designed to lead visitors along intellectual paths by means of meaningful juxtapositions, illustrations and schemes that provide a context for each specimen. A good museum is not a store of objects grouped by shape and size, but a planned disposition from which one can, again, feel that one is navigating through knowledge.

Objects displayed in museums, in temporary exhibitions, in botanical gardens and in zoos are just another form of documents (Latham, 2012). Kyle (1959, 19) has observed that poems or musical compositions are kept in libraries rather than museums due only to their material form, but are in principle no different from museum objects, inasmuch as they are 'something written about' rather than 'a writing about something'.

6.5 KO in the digital environment
6.5.1 Applying KO to digital documents
Nowadays another kind of collections is widely available: those of digital documents. These collections can cover many forms and formats, including texts, pictures, audiovisual materials, etc. As was noticed early on (Rayward, 1998), their digital nature makes all of them treatable and available in a unified way, through integrated interfaces.

Websites are themselves multimedia in nature, as a web page can easily embed texts, images, audio recordings or videos, all connected to related resources via networks of hypertextual links (Ridi, 2017). Projects selecting, archiving and providing a collection of good-quality digital resources are known as *digital libraries* – although they could just as well be called 'digital archives' or 'digital museums', given the integration made possible by such knowledge formats.

How should digital libraries, and digital collections more generally, be organized? A basic remark was expressed at the dawn of the computer age by the KO expert Brian Vickery (1960): despite its very different look, mechanized information such as punched cards (or, we can add, the more recent digital libraries, blogs and wikis) requires basically the same techniques as do paper documents so as to be structured and accessed in intellectually useful ways. These, quite simply, are the principles of KO that we have been describing throughout this book.

This idea may at first encounter some resistance, especially from those who have some economic interest in presenting their solutions as brand new tools. Commercial dynamics often produce new buzzwords (among which *taxonomy* and *ontology* may sometimes be included) to describe existing techniques that are merely adapted to the new technological context. While this can be part of the game, it is also important to acknowledge that the basic principles of KO provide the foundation for both old and new applications.

That said, KO principles obviously have to be applied in clever ways, rather than as blind-rule applications, in order to get the best combination of the mechanical power of computers and the intellectual power of KOSs.

The simplest, early way of applying KO to the internet has been the attribution of subject categories to websites. The very first development of the web as conceived by Tim Berners-Lee was indeed accompanied by the compilation of the WWW Virtual Library (section 5.3), a simple taxonomy where each category or subcategory links to a selection of web pages dealing with the corresponding topics. Many other subject gateways to internet resources have followed, some of which have also adopted such bibliographic KOSs as the UDC (Slavic, 2006). However, the huge proliferation of web resources has made human indexing of the whole internet a utopian aim.

Taxonomies still make sense for collections of selected resources, either general or in special domains. They are a key component in the profession of information architecture (IA), whose specialists design the structure of information content on websites or in other contexts of everyday life, trying to offer intuitive paths and make user navigation easy, always without losing the underlying structure (Resmini and Rosati, 2011). Another important application of taxonomies, as already noted, are Wikipedia categories.

In a more general view, after the great success of the brute power of search engines towards the end of the 1990s, in the 21st century there is an increasing awareness that further tools need to be developed so as to achieve what has been called a Semantic Web (as opposed, so to speak, to a purely 'Mechanical Web'). The KOSs and principles that are available from the rich heritage of library and information science are now increasingly acknowledged as important components of the Web of Data; their publication as linked open data is thus greatly encouraged and gradually progressing. We saw in Chapter 5 how this can be done in various formats for knowledge representation.

6.5.2 Problems and benefits of digital KO

From the perspective of KO, one advantage of digital documents is that words can be extracted from any section of them just by typing those words and launching a search. This is obviously simpler than having to browse a list of all relevant words in an alphabetical index, as was needed in traditional file cabinets. Not only does this allow for exploiting full texts – rather than only selected keywords – and indexing them automatically through bots; it also makes the search process easier.

The marvel of this new functionality has been greeted by many with exaggerated enthusiasm, as they believe that finding words inside texts makes all the traditional ordering methods obsolete. Why would we need indexes at all, if we can find information directly in any part of a document?

The fact is that the functions of knowledge-ordering techniques go beyond this. Indeed, as we have shown throughout this book, they especially consist in cognitive aids to explore available knowledge, as well as to organize search results. While alphabetical lists of words are no longer needed for most search applications (as it is quicker to just try to see whether or not a word gives relevant results, without any prior check for its presence in the index), systematic displays are still very useful facilities at both steps:

- for browsing available subjects along hierarchical and associative relationships until finding a suitable topic;
- for examining the results of a search organized in some meaningful way so as to select some of them or to get feedback leading to a new search.

To these ends, ordering and notations can still play a powerful part in our digital world, although many seem to have forgotten their techniques or believe that they are no longer needed. Of course, the richness of digital interfaces makes it possible to present captions (and their synonyms) as a more intuitive way to grasp the meaning and coverage of a category than esoteric symbols such as those of DDC or ILC may at first appear to be. On the other hand, the notation corresponding to each label can still be displayed as an additional tool, especially to suggest that the order presented is the result of a technical mechanism, the details of which do not necessarily have to be examined by casual users.

Expressive notations, where every additional digit means an additional rank of specificity (Gnoli, 2018c), are very suitable to be exploited in computers, where they allow not only for consistent ordering but also for truncated searches: e.g. show all DDC classmarks whose notation starts with 595.44, that is, all records labeled with the class of spiders or a subclass of it, that is, particular types of spiders; if you find too few of these, go up one rank and show all classmarks starting with 595.4 'arachnids', which can still include some relevant information; or show all classmarks including the DDC sub-string -09152- 'in forests' attached to any basic class, and so on.

However, the notations of most bibliographic classifications were conceived before the advent of computers, so that some details in them may need some adaptation to the new medium. Ranganathan's anteriorizing common isolates (see section 6.4) are expressed by an additional suffix that, in Ranganathan's conception, should be ordered before the corresponding basic class without any suffix. However, a basic ordering principle of computers is that 'no digit' comes before 'any digit', so some special script would need to be integrated into the interface to make such a sophisticated device of Colon Classification work properly. The same problem is encountered in ILC notation with spans, that is, sets of subclasses connected by W:

rsWu	Abrahamic religions
rs	Judaism
rt	Christianity
ru	Islam.

As spans are more general than the individual classes that they cover, they should be ordered before them. However, again, any suffix such as -Wu is ordered by computers after the basic class rs without suffix. In the ILC interface at www.iskoi.org/ilc/ this is solved by adding a hidden W to all notations, then ordering them, and finally removing the W in display. Such little adjustments are managed by PHP scripts and produce web pages where classes are ordered according to the correct principles of classification, as in the example above.

Apart from this unavoidable detail, the notation of ILC has been designed to suit computer orderings well, especially to use digits only from the basic ASCII character set, the international standard adopted by all operating systems, which includes in this order:

- most punctuation marks
- 0 to 9

- more punctuation marks (: ; < = > ? @)
- *A* to *Z*
- *a* to *z*.

Thus, for example, it is not by chance that in ILC, facet indicators are numerals and subclasses are letters, as the principles of faceted classification prescribe that facets are ordered before subclasses. Within subclasses, locally preferred classes *A–T* and other deictics, such as *U* 'the typical subclasses' or *X* 'any subclass', precede standard subclasses in *a–z*. Also, *z* never means a particular subclass but is used as an *emptying digit* (an invention of Ranganathan) to introduce further subclasses where more than 24 of them are needed:

tt modern nation states
ttb   Britain
...
ttc   Germany
ttczn Netherlands
ttczq Belgium
ttczx Luxembourg
ttd   France
...
tty   Argentina
ttyzc Chile.

As can be observed, shorter notations have been adopted for major countries that are expected to occur more commonly in indexing, thus adopting another trick invented by classificationist Zygmunt Dobrowolski (see Gnoli, 2018c, sect. 4.3).

6.5.3 Designing organized interfaces

Once a KOS is available, with its captions, synonyms, possibly a notation, etc., its structure and features should be taken into account in the user interfaces that have to leverage its power. Unfortunately, this is not often the case with currently existing library catalogs and other bibliographic tools, as has been shown in various surveys (Casson et al., 2011). Just taking a KOS and copying it into a database table without understanding its design and functionalities often means losing much of its power of organization.

A good interface should present a KOS structure in a clear way, distinguishing notation by captions, and synonyms by preferred terms. It should, especially, provide suitable hypertextual links that allow for navigation of its hierarchical trees and associative relationships. When presenting the results of a search, subject information should be displayed in a clear way, with links from every item to relaunch a search for further items indexed in the same way.

Indeed, as user studies and research by information architects have made clear, our common ways of searching for information are not just Boolean attempts of the kind 'find whether this information is there or not'. They include exploration by browsing and *berrypicking* (Bates, 2005), as well as a feedback process that leverages the results of a first search as additional information to conceive further, more refined searches. The creation of interfaces that connect such knowledge about users' behavior to the power of KOS structures, using all the devices available in graphical user interfaces, such as fonts, links, selection lists, radio buttons, flags, etc., is an art.

An example application is SciGator (http://scigator.unipv.it), a tool supplementing the standard search in the many libraries of the University of Pavia, which presents users with an adapted selection of the DDC classes that are most used in those libraries (Lardera et al., 2017). By accessing it, users can understand that a general scheme of knowledge is used (the one expressed in this KOS, clearly not the only possible one, but the one most used in the bibliographic records that are shared among Italian libraries). The hierarchical structure of DDC is shown clearly by indentations and links to subclasses. Related subclasses are also suggested on the right, so that users can be aware that, say, 627 hydraulic engineering is connected to 532 fluid dynamics as part of physics, a class available in a different part of the scheme.

Once a user has identified an appropriate class, searches in the university's OPAC can be launched in three ways: (1) only books having that class as their shelfmark, hence presumably focused on that class (say, hydraulic engineering); or (2) also books to which the class has been assigned as bibliographic information, although shelved in other classes or by local schemes; or (3) all the previous books plus those that have been assigned related classes, such as fluid dynamics. These three searches are presented in this sequence, so that users can start with the most focused and limited search, and only include larger sets in case the previous search has retrieved few or no relevant results. An additional functionality are buttons to launch the same search in the national SBN catalog, or in OCLC's international WorldCat, which include a much greater number of classified records that can be used as additional sources, or at least as bibliographic information without borrowing the corresponding documents from libraries located far away.

The case of a book dealing with both hydraulic engineering and the underlying fluid dynamics is a typical example of the possible coexistence in a document of several themes, of which one is identified by indexers as the base theme and others as particular themes (see section 3.4). As we saw in section 6.3.2, this book should be a primary result of searches for hydraulic engineering, while it should be listed only as a secondary suggestion as a result of searches for fluid dynamics.

To achieve this, a *double query* method has been proposed (Gnoli and Cheti, 2013): a search for fluid dynamics should launch a first query for all records classed with 532- or its subclasses as the leading term of a post-coordinated classmark or subject string (that is, as the base theme of documents); plus a second query for *[blank space]-532-* as an internal excerpt of the post-coordinated classmark string (that is, as only a particular theme). The results of the first query should be ranked higher than those of the second query, and shown with greater relevance, at the beginning of the results list. This would help users to identify results that are more relevant to them, before all other possibly related resources.

6.6 Conclusion

In this chapter we have reviewed some ways of applying the principles and techniques of KO to the management of real collections or documents, in any format. Indexing and retrieving knowledge items, independently of their format, is indeed a basic function of KO, as it focuses on intellectual content over accidental components such as being in a particular format or belonging to a particular collection. In other words, the dimension of phenomena that are dealt with in the document can be taken as primary, while those of perspectives, document forms, collections, information needs and people are only additional specifications.

Many automatic tools are now able to manage details about formats, languages, locations, etc., which belong to the document and collection dimensions. However, in order to index and exploit the dimensions of phenomena and of perspectives, intellectual work is still needed in most cases. KO, an ancient practice – although called by different names in the past (see section 1.4) – is thus a necessary companion to the more recently developed specialties of computer science and digital knowledge representation (see Chapter 5 and section 6.5).

Pragmatic principles may suggest how the most relevant sets of documents to be indexed intellectually can be selected, and which KOS types and indexing procedures best suit the contexts to hand. While systems of keywords and tags are simpler and can also be used by non-trained users to quickly provide information on the subject of large amounts of resources, more advanced systems such as thesauri, classifications or ontologies are needed to analyze and represent the content of most specialized resources and to serve users who are searching for it.

KO is a wide field, with a history rooted in both philosophy and information services. With the advent of new technologies, especially digital technologies, because these deal with its core object – information – KO has started to evolve and will continue to evolve. This does not mean that it should simply merge with knowledge representation techniques and computer science, as its special task of providing frameworks for knowledge contents and their exploration will always be needed.

Although many powerful tools are now available and there is a long history of ordering the sciences and their objects, our mission is to blend these two components in the best possible ways, so as to provide effective, comprehensive and up-to-date pictures of all that human knowledge has understood about our world up till now.

References

Araújo, P. C. de, Castanha, R. C. Gutierres and Hjørland, B. (2019) Citation index and indexing. In Hjørland, B. and Gnoli, C. (eds), *ISKO Encyclopedia of Knowledge Organization*, www.isko.org/cyclo/citation.

Austin, D. (1969) Prospects for a new general classification, *Journal of Librarianship*, 1 (3), 149–69.

Barité, M. (2018) Literary warrant. In Hjørland, B. and Gnoli, C. (eds), *ISKO Encyclopedia of Knowledge Organization*, www.isko.org/cyclo/literary_warrant. Version 1.0 *Knowledge Organization*, 45 (6), 517–36.

Bates, M. J. (2002) Toward an integrated model of information seeking and searching, *New Review of Information Behaviour Research*, 3, 1–15, https://pages.gseis.ucla.edu/faculty/bates/articles/info_SeekSearch-i-030329.html.

Bates, M. J. (2005) Berrypicking. In Fisher, K. E., Erdelez, S. and McKechnie, L. (eds), *Theories of Information Behavior*, Information Today, 58–62.

Bawden, D. and Robinson, L. (2012) *Introduction to Information Science*, Facet.

Bawden, D. and Robinson, L. (2015) Information and the gaining of understanding, *Journal of Information Science*, 42 (3), 294–9.

Bawden, D. and Robinson, L. (2017) Curating the infosphere: Luciano Floridi's Philosophy of Information as the foundation for library and information science, *Journal of Documentation*, 74 (1), 2–17.

Beghtol, C. (1998) Knowledge domains: multidisciplinary and bibliographic classification systems, *Knowledge Organization*, 25 (1/2), 1–12.

Beghtol, C. (2002) A proposed ethical warrant for knowledge representation and organization systems, *Journal of Documentation*, 58 (5), 507–32.

Beghtol, C. (2003) Classification for information retrieval and classification for knowledge discovery: relationships between 'professional' and 'naïve' classification, *Knowledge Organization*, 30 (2), 64–73.

Begthol, C. (2004) Exploring new approaches to the organization of knowledge: the Subject Classification of James Duff Brown, *Library Trends*, 52 (4), 702–18, www.ideals.illinois.edu/handle/2142/1694.

Berlin, B. and Kay, P. (1969) *Basic color terms: their universality and evolution*, University of California Press.

Bhattacharyya, G. (1982) Classaurus: its fundamentals, design and use. In Dahlberg, I. (ed.), *Universal Classification: subject analysis and ordering systems: proceedings of the 4th International Study Conference on Classification Research – 6th Annual Conference of Gesellschaft für Klassifikation, Augsburg, 28 June–2 July 1982*, Indeks, vol. 1, 139–48.

Bhattacharyya, G. and Ranganathan, S. R. (1974) From knowledge classification to library classification. In Wojciechowski, J. A. (ed.), *Conceptual Basis of the Classification of Knowledge: proceedings of the Ottawa conference, 1–5 October 1971*, 119–43, Verlag Dokumentation.

Bianchini, C., Gnoli, C. and Giusti, L. (2017) The APUPA bell curve: Ranganathan's visual pattern for knowledge organization, *Les cahiers du numérique*, **13** (1), 49–68.

Blair, D. C. (1980) Searching biases in large interactive document retrieval systems, *Journal of the American Society for Information Science*, **31** (4), 271–7.

Bliss, H. E. (1929) *The Organization of Knowledge and the System of the Sciences*, Holt.

Bliss, H. E. (1933) *The Organization of Knowledge in Libraries*, Wilson.

Bloch, M. (1952) *Apologie pour l'histoire ou Métier d'historien*, 2nd edn, Colin, éd. électronique Chicoutimi 2005, http://classiques.uqac.ca/classiques/bloch_marc/apologie_histoire/bloch_apologie.pdf.

Borges, J. L. (1952) El idioma analitico de John Wilkins. In *Otras inquisiciones (1937–1952)*, Sur.

Bragato Barros, T. E. (ed.) (2019) Special issue on archival knowledge organization, *Knowledge Organization*, **46** (7), 493–568.

Briet, S. (1951) *Qu'est-ce que la documentation?* Edit.

Broughton, V. (2000) A new classification for the literature of religion. In *Proceedings of 66th IFLA Council and General Conference, Jerusalem, 13–18 August 2000*, https://archive.ifla.org/IV/ifla66/papers/034-130e.htm. Also in *International Cataloguing and Bibliographic Control*, **29** (4).

Broughton, V. (2011) Facet analysis as a tool for modelling subject domains and terminologies. In Slavic, A. and Civallero, E. (eds), *Classification and Ontology: formal approaches and access to knowledge: proceedings of the International UDC Seminar, 19–20 September 2011, The Hague*, Ergon, 207–28.

Bu, S. (2017) Chinese Library Classification (CLC), translated by Wei Fan. In Hjørland, B. and Gnoli, C. (eds), *ISKO Encyclopedia of Knowledge Organization*, www.isko.org/cyclo/clc.

Buckland, M. (2014) Documentality beyond documents, *The Monist*, **97** (2), 179–86.

Buckland, M. (2018) Document theory. In Hjørland, B. and Gnoli, C. (eds), *ISKO Encyclopedia of Knowledge Organization*, www.isko.org/cyclo/document. Version 1.0 *Knowledge Organization*, **45** (5), 425–36.

Campbell, G. (2004) A queer eye for the faceted guy: how a universal classification principle can be applied to a distinct subculture. In McIlwaine, I. C. (ed.), *Knowledge Organization and the Global Information Society: Proceedings 8th*

International ISKO Conference, London, 13–16 July 2004, Ergon, 109–13.

Casson, E., Fabbrizzi, A. and Slavic, A. (2011) Subject search in Italian OPACs: an opportunity in waiting? In Landry, P., Bultrini, L., O'Neill, E. T. and Roe, S. K. (eds), *Subject Access: preparing for the future*, De Gruyter Saur, 37–50.

Cheti, A. (1996) *Manuale ipertestuale di analisi concettuale*, realisator Serena Spinelli, University of Bologna, www2.sba.unibo.it/miac/.

Choi, I. (2017) Visualizations of cross-cultural bibliographic classification: comparative studies of the Korean Decimal Classification and the Dewey Decimal Classification, *Proceedings from North American Symposium on Knowledge Organization*, 6, http://journals.lib.washington.edu/index.php/nasko/article/view/15229.

Comte, A. (1854) *Système de politique positive*, Carilian-Goeury et Dalmont.

CRG: Classification Research Group (1955) The need for a faceted classification as the basis for all methods of information retrieval, *Library Association Record*, 57 (7), 262–8.

CRG: Classification Research Group (1978) CRG Bulletin 11, *Journal of Documentation*, 34 (1), 23.

Dahlberg, I. (1974) *Grundlagen universaler Wissensordnung*, Verlag Dokumentation.

Dahlberg, I. (1978) A referent-oriented, analytical concept theory for Inter-Concept, *International Classification*, 5 (3), 142–51.

DCMI (2012) *Dublin Core Metadata Element Set*, Version 1.1. Reference Description, https://www.dublincore.org/specifications/dublin-core/dces/.

Dextre Clarke, S. (2017) Thesaurus (for information retrieval). In Hjørland, B. and Gnoli, C. (eds), *ISKO Encyclopedia of Knowledge Organization*, www.isko.org/cyclo/thesaurus.

Dextre Clarke, S. and Vernau, J. (eds) (2016) Special issue: The Great Debate: 'This house believes that the traditional thesaurus has no place in modern information retrieval', *Knowledge Organization*, 43 (3).

Diderot, D. (1755) Encyclopédie. In *Encyclopédie ou Dictionnaire raisonné des sciences, des arts et des métiers*, vol. 5, 635–48, translated by Philip Stewart, Michigan Publishing, 2002, https://quod.lib.umich.edu/d/did/.

Dousa, T. M. (2009) Evolutionary order in the classification theories of C. A. Cutter and E. C. Richardson: its nature and limits, *Proceedings from North American Symposium on Knowledge Organization*, 2, https://journals.lib.washington.edu/index.php/nasko/article/view/12810.

Dousa, T. M. (2018) Library Classification, Part 1: introduction and premodern classification. In Hjørland, B. and Gnoli, C. (eds), *ISKO Encyclopedia of Knowledge Organization*, www.isko.org/cyclo/library_classification.

Dousa, T. M. and Ibekwe-San Juan, F. (2014) Epistemological and methodological eclecticism in the construction of knowledge organization systems (KOSs): the case of analytico-synthetic KOSs. In Babik, W. (ed.), *Knowledge Organization in the 21st*

Century: between historical patterns and future prospects: proceedings Thirteenth ISKO Conference, Krakow, 19–22 May 2014, Ergon, 152–9.

Doyle, A. M. and Metoyer, C. A. (eds) (2015) Indigenous knowledge organization: special issue, *Cataloging & Classification Quarterly*, **53** (5–6).

Dunn, H. and Bourcier, P. (2019) Nomenclature for museum cataloging. In Hjørland, B. and Gnoli, C. (eds), *ISKO Encyclopedia of Knowledge Organization*, www.isko.org/cyclo/nomenclature.

Durand de Gros, J. M. (1899) *Aperçus de taxinomie générale*, Alcan.

Egan, M. E. and Shera, J. H. (1952) Foundations of a theory of bibliography, *Library Quarterly*, **22** (2), 125–37.

Emunds, H. (1976) Bericht zur Lage der dreigeteilten Bibliothek, *Buch und Bibliothek*, **28** (4), 269–88.

Fabbrizzi, A. (2014) An atlas of classification: signage between open shelves, the Web and the catalogue, *JLIS.it*, **5** (2), 101–22, www.jlis.it/article/view/10068.

Farradane, J. E. L. (1950) A scientific theory of classification and indexing and its practical applications, *Journal of Documentation*, **6** (2), 83–92.

Feinberg, M. (2011) Expressive bibliography: personal collections in public space, *Knowledge Organization*, **38** (2), 123–34.

Floridi, L. (2002) On defining library and information science as applied philosophy of information, *Social Epistemology*, **16** (1), 37–49.

Floridi, L. (2010) *Information: a very short introduction*, Oxford University Press.

Floridi, L. (2019) *The Logic of Information: a theory of philosophy as conceptual design*, Oxford University Press.

Foskett, D. J. (1958) *Library Classification and the Field of Knowledge*, Chaucer House.

Foskett, D. J. (1972) Information and general systems theory, *Journal of Librarianship*, **4** (3), 205–9.

Foskett, D. J. (1991) Concerning general and special classifications, *International Classification*, **18** (2), 87–91.

Foucault, M. (1972) *The Archaeology of Knowledge*, Tavistock.

Fraser, C. (2019) Mathematics in classification systems. In Hjørland, B. and Gnoli, C. (eds), *ISKO Encyclopedia of Knowledge Organization*, www.isko.org/cyclo/mathematics.

French, S. (2014) *The Structure of the World: metaphysics and representation*, Oxford University Press.

Frické, M. (2016) Logical division. In Hjørland, B. and Gnoli, C. (eds), *ISKO Encyclopedia of Knowledge Organization*, www.isko.org/cyclo/dikw. Version 1.0 *Knowledge Organization*, **43**, 7, 539–49.

Frické, M. (2018) The knowledge pyramid: the DIKW hierarchy. In Hjørland, B. and Gnoli, C. (eds), *ISKO Encyclopedia of Knowledge Organization*, www.isko.org/cyclo/dikw. Version 1.0 *Knowledge Organization*, **49** (1), 2019, 33–46.

Gardiner, J. (1947) *Ancient Egyptian Onomastica*, Oxford University Press.

Gatto, E. (2006) A righe o a quadretti?... In *Le dimensioni dell'informazione: giornata di studio AIB Piemonte-ISKO Italia, Torino, 12 giugno 2004,* www.iskoi.org/doc/dimensioni4.htm.

Gnoli, C. (2010) Classification transcends library business, *Knowledge Organization,* **37** (3), 223–9.

Gnoli, C. (2016) Classifying phenomena, part 1: Dimensions, *Knowledge Organization,* **43** (6), 403–15.

Gnoli, C. (2018a) Genealogical classification. In Hjørland, B. and Gnoli, C. (eds), *ISKO Encyclopedia of Knowledge Organization,* www.isko.org/cyclo/genealogical.

Gnoli, C. (2018b) Mentefacts as a missing level in information theory, *Journal of Documentation,* **74** (6), 1226–42.

Gnoli, C. (2018c) Notation. In Hjørland, B. and Gnoli, C. (eds), *ISKO Encyclopedia of Knowledge Organization,* www.isko.org/cyclo/notation. Version 1 *Knowledge Organization,* **45**, 8, 667–84.

Gnoli, C. and Cheti, A. (2013) Sorting documents by base theme with synthetic classification: the double query method. In Slavic, A., Akdag Salah, A. and Davies, S. (eds), *Classification and Visualization: interfaces to knowledge: proceedings International UDC Seminar, The Hague, 24–25 October 2013,* Ergon, 225–32.

Gnoli, C., Pullmann, T., Cousson, P., Merli, G. and Szostak, R. (2011) Representing the structural elements of a freely faceted classification. In Slavic, A. and Civallero, E. (eds), *Classification and Ontology: formal approaches and access to knowledge: proceedings International UDC Seminar, The Hague, 19–20 September 2011,* Ergon, 193–206.

Golub, K. (2015) *Subject Access to Information: an interdisciplinary approach,* Libraries Unlimited.

Golub, K. (2017) Automatic subject indexing of text. In Hjørland, B. and Gnoli, C. (eds), *ISKO Encyclopedia of Knowledge Organization,* www.isko.org/cyclo/automatic. Version 1.1 *Knowledge Organization,* **46** (2), 104–21.

Golub, K., Lykke, M. and Tudhope, D. (2014) Enhancing social tagging with automated keywords from the Dewey Decimal Classification, *Journal of Documentation,* **70**, 801–28.

Gorman, M. (2003) Cataloguing in an electronic age, *Cataloging & Classification Quarterly,* **36** (3–4), 5–17.

Goody, J. (1977) *The Domestication of the Savage Mind,* Cambridge University.

Grolier, É. de (1974) Le système des sciences et l'evolution du savoir. In Wojciechowski, J. A. (ed.), *Conceptual Bases of the Classification of Knowledge: proceedings of the Ottawa conference, 1–5 October 1971,* Verlag Dokumentation, 20–118.

Grolier, É. de (1982) Classification as cultural artefacts. In Dahlberg, I. (ed.), *Universal Classification: subject analysis and ordering system: proceedings 4th*

International Study Conference on Classification Research, Augsburg, 1982, Indeks, Vol 1, 19–34.

Hartel, J. and Hjørland, B. (2003) Afterword: ontological, epistemological and sociological dimensions of domains, *Knowledge Organization*, **30** (3–4), 239–45.

Hartmann, N. (1953) *New Ways of Ontology*, Regnery. German edn: *Neue Wege der Ontologie*, Kohlhammer, 1949, available at: https://archive.org/details/newwaysofontolog00hart.

Hedden, H. (2016) *The Accidental Taxonomist*, 2nd edn, Information Today.

Hjørland, B. (2012) Knowledge organization = information organization? In Neelameghan, A. and Raghavan, K. S. (eds), *Categories, Contexts and Relations in Knowledge Organization: proceedings Twelfth International ISKO Conference, Mysore, 6–9 August 2012*, Ergon, 8–14.

Hjørland, B. (2013), User-based and cognitive approaches to knowledge organization: a theoretical analysis of the research literature, *Knowledge Organization*, **40** (1), 11–27. Republished in *ISKO Encyclopedia of Knowledge Organization*, www.isko.org/cyclo/user_based, 2018.

Hjørland, B. (2016) The paradox of atheoretical classification, *Knowledge Organization*, **43** (5), 313–23.

Hjørland, B. (2017a) Classification. In Hjørland, B. and Gnoli, C. (eds), *ISKO Encyclopedia of Knowledge Organization*, www.isko.org/cyclo/classification. Version 1.0 *Knowledge Organization*, **44** (2), 97–128.

Hjørland, B. (2017b) Domain analysis. In Hjørland, B. and Gnoli, C. (eds), *ISKO Encyclopedia of Knowledge Organization*, www.isko.org/cyclo/domain_analysis. Version 1.0 *Knowledge Organization*, **44** (6), 436–64.

Hjørland, B. (2017c) Library and information science (LIS). In Hjørland, B. and Gnoli, C. (eds), *ISKO Encyclopedia of Knowledge Organization*, www.isko.org/cyclo/lis. Version 1.0 *Knowledge Organization*, **45** (3), 232–54 and **45** (4), 319–38.

Hjørland, B. and Nicolaisen, J. (2004) Scientific and scholarly classifications are not "naïve": a comment to Begthol (2003), *Knowledge Organization*, **31** (1), 55–61.

Hudon, M. (2019) Facet. In Hjørland, B. and Gnoli, C. (eds), *ISKO Encyclopedia of Knowledge Organization*, www.isko.org/cyclo/facet.

Hulme, E. W. (1911) Principles of book classification, Chapter III: On the definition of class headings, and the natural limit to the extension of book classification, *Library Association Record*, **13**, 444–9.

Hutchins, W. J. (1975) *Languages of Indexing and Classification*, Peregrinus.

Hyman, R. (1982) *Shelf Access in Libraries*, American Library Association.

Iommi, S. (2019) *Epifania del vedere negato: il mondo agropastorale nel documentario corto italiano, 1939–1969*, Diabasis.

ISKO Italia (2007) *The León Manifesto*, www.iskoi.org/ilc/leon.php. Republished in *Knowledge Organization*, **34** (1), 6–8.

Jacob, E. K. (1994) Classification and crossdisciplinary communication: breaching the boundaries imposed by classificatory structure. In Albrechtsen, H. and Ørnager, S. (eds), *Knowledge Organization and Quality Management: proceedings Third International ISKO Conference, Copenhagen, 20–24 June 1994*, Indeks, 101–8.

Johansson, S. and Golub, K. (2019) LibraryThing for libraries: how tag moderation and size limitations affect tag clouds, *Knowledge Organization*, **46** (4), 245–59.

Kleineberg, M. (2017) Integrative levels. In Hjørland, B. and Gnoli, C. (eds), *ISKO Encyclopedia of Knowledge Organization*, www.isko.org/cyclo/integrative_levels. Version 1.0 *Knowledge Organization*, **44** (5), 349–79.

Korwin, W. and Kund, H. (2019) Alphabetization. In Hjørland, B. and Gnoli, C. (eds), *ISKO Encyclopedia of Knowledge Organization*, www.isko.org/cyclo/alphabetization.

Krug, S. (2014) *Don't Make Me Think, Revisited: a common sense approach to Web usability*, 3rd edn, New Riders.

Kwasnik, B. H. and Rubin, V. (2003) Stretching conceptual structures in classifications across languages and cultures, *Cataloging & Classification Quarterly*, **37** (1–2), 33–47.

Kyle, B. (1959) An examination of some problems involved in drafting general classifications and some proposals for their solution, *Revue de la documentation*, **26** (1), 17–21.

La Barre, K. (2017) Interrogating facet theory: decolonizing knowledge organization. In Smiraglia, R. P. and Lee, H.-L. (eds), *Dimensions of Knowledge: facets for knowledge organization*, Ergon.

Laporte, S. (2017) Ideal language. In Hjørland, B. and Gnoli, C. (eds), *ISKO Encyclopedia of Knowledge Organization*, www.isko.org/cyclo/ideal_language. Version 1.0 *Knowledge Organization*, **45** (7), 586–608.

Lardera, M., Gnoli, C., Rolandi, C. and Trzmielewski, M. (2017) Developing SciGator, a DDC-based library browsing tool, *Knowledge Organization*, **44** (8), 638–43.

Latham, K. F. (2012) Museum object as document, *Journal of Documentation*, **68** (1), 45–71.

Lee, D. (2018) Hornbostel Sachs classification. In Hjørland, B. and Gnoli, C. (eds), *ISKO Encyclopedia of Knowledge Organization*, www.isko.org/cyclo/hornbostel.

Lee, D., Robinson, L. and Bawden, D. (2019) Modelling the relationship between scientific and bibliographic classification for music, *Journal of the Association for Information Science and Technology*, **70** (3), 230–41.

López-Huertas, M. J. (2013) Reflexions on multidimensional knowledge: its influence on the foundation of knowledge organization, *Knowledge Organization*, **40** (6), 400–7.

Lorenz, K. Z. (1973) *Behind the Mirror: a search for a natural history of human knowledge*, Harcourt Brace Jovanovich.

Maat, J. (2004) *Philosophical Languages in the Seventeenth Century: Dalgarno, Wilkins, Leibniz*, Kluwer.

Marshall, B. (2013) tweet, 4 December 2013, *Twitter*,
    https://twitter.com/flowchainsensei/status/408167162344648704.
Matthews, B., Jones, C., Puzo , B., Moon, J., Tudhope, D., Golub, K. and Lykke
    Nielsen, M. (2010) An evaluation of enhancing social tagging with a knowledge
    organization system, *ASLIB Proceedings* **62** (4–5), 447–65.
Mayr, P. and Scharnhorst, A. (2015) Combining bibliometrics and information retrieval:
    preface, *Scientometrics*, **102** (3), 2191–2.
McIlwaine, I. C. (2004) A question of place. In McIlwaine, I. C. (ed.), *Knowledge
    Organization and the Global Information Society: proceedings Eighth International
    ISKO Conference, London, 13–16 July 2004*, Ergon, 179–85.
Miller, G. A. (1956) The magical number seven, plus or minus two: some limits on our
    capacity for processing information, *Psychological Review*, **63** (2), 81–97.
Mills, J. and Broughton, V. (1977) *Bliss Bibliographic Classification, second edition.
    Introduction and auxiliary schedules*, Butterworths.
Nagel, T. (1986) *The View from Nowhere*, Oxford University Press.
Ohly, H. P. (2018) Ingetraut Dahlberg. In Hjørland, B. and Gnoli, C. (eds), *ISKO
    Encyclopedia of Knowledge Organization*, www.isko.org/cyclo/dahlberg.
Olson, H. A. (2002) *The Power to Name: locating the limits of subject representation in
    libraries*, Springer.
Olson, H. A. (2010) Earthly order and the oneness of mysticism: Hugh of Saint Victor
    and medieval classification of wisdom, *Knowledge Organization*, **37** (2), 121–38.
Ong, W. (1982) *Orality and Literacy: the technologizing of the word*, Methuen.
Ong, W. (1983) *Ramus: method, and the decay of dialogue*. The University of Chicago
    Press.
Otlet, P. (1934) *Traité de documentation: le livre sur le livre: théorie et pratique*,
    Mundaneum.
Pagès, R. (1948) Transformations documentaires et milieu culturel: essai de
    documentologie, *Review of Documentation*, **15** (3), 53–64.
Peirce, C. S. (1934) *Collected Papers*, ed. Hartshorn, C. and Weiss, P., vol. 5, Harvard
    University Press.
Piaget, J. (1953) *The Origin of Intelligence in the Child*, Routledge & Kegan Paul.
Popper, K. R. (1978) Three worlds: the Tanner lecture on human values, delivered at
    the University of Michigan, 7 April,
    https://tannerlectures.utah.edu/_documents/a-to-z/p/popper80.pdf.
Poli, R. (1996) Ontology for knowledge organization. In Green, R. (ed.), *Knowledge
    Organization and Change: proceedings Fourth International ISKO Conference,
    Washington, DC, 15–18 July 1996*, Indeks, 313–9.
Poli, R. (2001) The basic problem of the theory of levels of reality, *Axiomathes*, **12**,
    261–83.
Quintarelli, E. (2005) Folksonomies: power to the people. In *ISKO Italy-UniMIB
    Meeting, Milan, 24 June 2005*, www.iskoi.org/doc/folksonomies.htm.

Raieli, R. (2013) *Multimedia Information Retrieval: theory and techniques*, Chandos.

Ranganathan, S. R. (1967). *Prolegomena to Library Classification*, 3rd edn, Asia Publishing House. Also available through University of Arizona, https://repository.arizona.edu/handle/10150/106370.

Rayward, W. B. (1998) Electronic information and the functional integration of libraries, museums, and archives. In Higgs, E. (ed.), *History and Electronic Artefacts*, Oxford University Press, 207–26.

Resmini, A. and Rosati, L. (2011) *Pervasive Information Architecture: designing cross-channel user experiences*, Morgan Kaufmann.

Ridi, R. (2013) Ethical values for knowledge organization, *Knowledge Organization*, **40** (3), 187–96.

Ridi, R. (2017) Hypertext. In Hjørland, B. and Gnoli, C. (eds), *ISKO Encyclopedia of Knowledge Organization*, www.isko.org/cyclo/hypertext. Version 1.0 *Knowledge Organization*, **45** (5), 393–424.

Rogers, B. (2017) *Perception: a very short introduction*, Oxford University Press.

Rossi, P. (2000) *Clavis universalis: arti della memoria e logica combinatoria da Lullo a Leibniz*, 3a ed., il Mulino. English translation of 2nd ed.: *Logic and the Art of Memory: the quest for a universal language*, University of Chicago Press, 2000.

Rowley, J. E. (2007) The wisdom hierarchy: representations of the DIKW hierarchy, *Journal of Information Science*, **33** (2), 163–80.

Sales, R. de and Pires, T. B. (2017) The classification of Harris: influences of Bacon and Hegel in the universe of library classification, *Proceedings 6th North American Symposium of Knowledge Organization*, Champaign, https://pdfs.semanticscholar.org/3510/8c6021b3409db0de8ee3c7c0977699b6bccc.pdf.

Santoro, M. (2015) Per una storia delle classificazioni bibliografiche. 1: Introduzione; Le origini: Mesopotamia ed Egitto, *Bibliotime*, **17** (1), www.aib.it/aib/sezioni/emr/bibtime/num-xvii-1/santoro.htm.

Satija, M. P. (2017) Colon Classification (CC). In Hjørland, B. and Gnoli, C. (eds), *ISKO Encyclopedia of Knowledge Organization*, www.isko.org/cyclo/colon_classification. Version 2.0 *Knowledge Organization*, **44** (4), 291–307.

Slavic, A. (2006) UDC in subject gateways: experiment or opportunity? *Knowledge Organization*, **33** (2), 67–85.

Slavic, A. and Civallero, E. (eds) (2011) *Classification and Ontology: formal approaches and access to knowledge: proceedings of the International UDC Seminar, 19–20 September 2011, The Hague*, Ergon.

Soergel, D. (2014) Knowledge organization for learning. In Babik, W. (ed.), *Knowledge Organization in the 21st Century: between historical patterns and future prospects: proceedings Thirteenth ISKO Conference, Krakow, 19–22 May 2014*, Ergon, 22–32.

Soergel, D. (2015) Unleashing the power of data through organization: structure and connections for meaning, learning and discovery, *Knowledge Organization*, **42** (6), 401–27.

Sowa, J. F. (1999) *Knowledge Representation: logical, philosophical, and computational foundations*, Brooks Cole.

Spärck Jones, K. (1972) A statistical interpretation of term specificity and its application in retrieval, *Journal of Documentation*, **28** (1), 11–21.

Stevenson, G. (1978) Andreas Schleiermacher's Bibliographic Classification and its relationship to the Dewey Decimal and Library of Congress classifications, *University of Illinois Graduate School of Library Science Occasional Papers*, **136**, http://hdl.handle.net/2142/3798.

Sukyasian, E. (2017) Library-Bibliographical Classification (LBC). In Hjørland, B. and Gnoli, C. (eds), *ISKO Encyclopedia of Knowledge Organization*, www.isko.org/cyclo/lbc.

Swanson, D. R. (1986) Undiscovered public knowledge, *Library Quarterly*, **56** (2), 103–18.

Szostak, R. (2008) Classification, interdisciplinarity, and the study of science, *Journal of Documentation*, **64** (3), 319–32.

Szostak, R., Gnoli, C. and López-Huertas, M. (2016) *Interdisciplinary Knowledge Organization*, Springer.

Tennis, J. T. (2002) Subject ontogeny: subject access through time and the dimensionality of classification. In López-Huertas, M. J. (ed.), *Challenges in Knowledge Representation and Organization for the 21st Century: integration of knowledge across boundaries: proceedings Seventh International ISKO Conference, 2002*, Ergon, 54–9, https://papers.ssrn.com/sol3/papers.cfm?abstract_id=2879017.

Tennis, J. T. (ed.) (2014) 25th ASIS SIG/CR Classification Research Workshop, *Advances in Classification Research Online*, https://journals.lib.washington.edu/index.php/acro/issue/view/1041.

Tognoli, N. Bolfarini and Guimarães, J. A. Chaves (2018) Provenance. In Hjørland, B. and Gnoli, C. (eds), *ISKO Encyclopedia of Knowledge Organization*, www.isko.org/cyclo/provenance.

Verdin, K. L. and Verdin, J. P. (1999) A topological system for delineation and codification of the Earth's river basins, *Journal of Hydrology*, **218** (1–2), 1–12.

Vickery, B. C. (1953) The significance of John Wilkins in the history of bibliographical classification, *Libri*, **2**, 326–43.

Vickery, B. C. (1960) *Faceted Classification: a guide to construction and use of special schemes*, Association of Special Libraries and Information Bureaux.

Vickery, B. C. (2008) The structure of subject classifications for document retrieval. In *Brian Vickery at home*, www.lucis.me.uk (closed). Republished in *Integrative Levels Classification*, www.iskoi.org/ilc/vickery.php, 2010.

W3C (2004a) *SKOS, Simple Knowledge Organization System*,
www.w3.org/2004/02/skos/.

W3C (2004b) *OWL, Web Ontology Language. Guide*, www.w3.org/TR/owl-guide/.

Zeng, M., Panzer, M. and Salaba, A. (2010) Expressing classification schemes with
OWL2: exploring issues and opportunities based on experiments using OWL 2 for
three classification schemes. In Gnoli, C. and Mazzocchi, F. (eds), *Paradigms and
Conceptual Systems in Knowledge Organization: proceedings Eleventh International
ISKO Conference, Rome, 23–26 February 2010*, Ergon, 356–62.

Index